ADVANCE PRAISE FOR

Classrooms in the Real World

Dr. Scott Mandel is an accomplished teacher. His new book allows him to combine his experiences, insights and humor in a manner which permits him to share an array of practical suggestions for classroom teachers. Most memorable among his tools, tips and timesavers:

- Be an advocate for your students
- Correct the behavior—not the student
- Leave your ego at the door

These and other tips are interwoven with personal observations and memories. A valuable resource for both veteran and novice educators!

Peggy Taylor Presley, Director, Human Resources Division: Teacher Support and Development Program

The best way to know where you're headed is to understand where you've been. In this volume of lively anecdotes, Dr. Mandel sends us snapshots of his experiences in the classroom, and then delves into how what he's learned applies to teaching today. Veteran teachers will nod their heads and grin as they think, "We really used to do that, didn't we?" For educators just joining the ranks, this book has even more value—Dr. Mandel provides a roadmap for what to do (and what not to do), but more importantly, he shines a guiding light on what is possible in the future of education.

Brian Muller, Specialist, Peer Assistance and Review Program; Former Advisor for District Intern Program; Former Secondary Teacher

With a collection of relatable and applicable stories, *Classrooms in the Real World* illustrates the delicate balance between following one's instincts as an educator, and meeting the modern requirements of the job. Dr. Mandel shows that a good teacher does what she believes will excite and inspire students. This book is invaluable to a both novice and veteran teachers who find themselves being pulled in different directions by students, colleagues, administrators, district officials, researchers, and their own guts.

Amanda Corr, Second Year Teacher

Dr. Mandel's latest offering is a must-read. Whether you are a veteran teacher, wet behind the ears, or somewhere in between, this is the book for you! His sound and practical advice, wrapped in layers of skillfully spun memories from his long career, will make you laugh, think, and probably come away with at least one ah ha! moment for your own practice.

Abigail Abbott-Perez, Veteran Secondary Teacher

Dr. Mandel presents snapshots of his most authentic teaching moments and experiences. He takes you on a journey into what teaching is really like. As a veteran educator, Mandel gives you practical advice and insider tips to help navigate through the complex and unpredictable nature of the teaching profession. This book is an insightful read for new teachers and anyone wondering what it's really like to be a teacher.

Leila Shapiro, Veteran Elementary Teacher

Classrooms in the Real World

Classrooms in the Real World

Practical Advice from a Veteran Teacher

SCOTT MANDEL

Myers Education Press

GORHAM, MAINE

Published by Myers Education Press, LLC

P.O. Box 424, Gorham, ME 04038

Myers Education Press is an academic publisher specializing in books, e-books, and digital content in the field of education. All of our books are subjected to a rigorous peer review process and produced in compliance with the standards of the Council on Library and Information Resources.

Library of Congress Cataloging-in-Publication Data available from Library of Congress.

13-digit ISBN 978-1-9755-0335-2 (paperback)
13-digit ISBN 978-1-9755-0334-5 (hardcover)
13-digit ISBN 978-1-9755-0336-9 (library networkable e-edition)
13-digit ISBN 978-1-9755-0337-6 (consumer e-edition)

Printed in the United States of America.

All first editions printed on acid-free paper that meets the American National Standards Institute Z39-48 standard.

Books published by Myers Education Press may be purchased at special quantity discount rates for groups, workshops, training organizations, and classroom usage. Please call our customer service department at 1-800-232-0223 for details.

Cover and interior design by Sophie Appel

Visit us on the web at **www.myersedpress.com** to browse our complete list of titles.

FOLLIES

Contents

Acknowledgments

It's impossible to put together a successful book without the assistance of a lot of talented people. First, I need to thank four awesome teachers who donated their time to read, edit, comment, and lead me through these pages: Carl Dugas, Melodie Bitter, Dr. Rob Schuck, and LoriAnne Denne. Thank you all—I couldn't have completed this book without you.

Second, I want to thank the wonderful people at Myers Education Press, starting with Chris Myers, who invited me into the Myers publishing family, as well as Stephanie Gabaree and Emily Janson.

My Motto of Life and the Dedication Associated with It

Everyone should have a motto—something that exemplifies their basic concept of life and the world. As a teacher, it also helps to have one that guides your daily life in the classroom. Mine came from a very good friend and one of my "heroes":

> Love is Good. Hate is Bad. See you tomorrow.

This book is dedicated to John Jacobson, the founder of America Sings! and a life-long educator in the arts.

Jewish legend says that when the world was created, God placed ten *tzaddiks*, the ultimate righteous, specially good people, on the earth. And that throughout time, as one passed away, another took his place. As long as ten *tzaddiks* remained on earth, evil would be kept at bay.

I believe that John Jacobson is one of those *tzaddiks*.

For over twenty-five years, John has provided the America Sings! experience to students around the world. His goals, as stated on the *americasings.org* website, are:

- To educate young people about the joys of philanthropy and their opportunities for charitable service and giving.

- To provide high-quality, non-competitive performing opportunities for young singers and dancers from choral organizations.
- To make direct contributions on behalf of these young choral performers to established children's charities, especially donations for disadvantaged children.
- To promote throughout the nation's schools and the national media a positive image of American youth involved in public service to needy children through the performing arts.
- To promote and stimulate interest in choral music as an art form among young people and the general public as a whole.

My singers have participated almost every year since Festival #10.

But John's influence goes well beyond that. He inspires kids. He inspires teachers. For anyone who has met him, or participated in one of his festivals, or read one of his books, he makes all of us want to improve the world through our music. He tries to enable us to use our talents, and the talents of our students, for the betterment of society.

In his final talk of the day at a recent John Jacobson Choreography Workshop, an annual summer event that I attend with my choreographers, he related how his father regularly shared this special philosophy of life:

> Love is Good. Hate is Bad. See you tomorrow.

It struck me as the ultimate philosophy of life. Accentuate the positive, avoid the negative, and know that we will see each other again. That day, I fell in love with the saying.

And so, when I was formulating this book of stories from my life's experiences, I could think of no better way to begin explaining my philosophy.

I hope John doesn't mind that I'm using it.

To close, and most appropriately for those who know me, I want to quote some of the most famous words ever used in a musical. Adapted from the climax of the Broadway show *Wicked*:

> "Who can say if we've been changed for the better, but because we knew John, our lives have been changed, for good."

Introduction—Why Am I Writing This Book?

When I started my thirtieth year (sigh) in a Los Angeles classroom a number of years ago, I looked around my school and asked myself, "What have I done with my life?" A very frightening question.

I understood my "professional worth" as I watched my students grow throughout the year—especially my eighth graders, whom I knew as little "babies" when they started sixth grade. That's my favorite part of teaching middle school—being able to watch my kids grow.

But why sit down and write a book about it?

Actually, the idea came to me over the past year. I've taught teacher salary point classes every year, and I regularly present professional development workshops. Now, in my Saturday teacher classes—and I'm sure you will notice this tendency as you read this book—I go off on tangents quite regularly. Mostly I tell stories: examples from my teaching over the past 3+ decades. Sometimes I share specific teaching/curricular ideas that I've learned over the years, stuff that is not normally found in teacher education books. Most of the participants enjoy these anecdotes and teaching tips—usually more than the curricular material I'm presenting! And for those who are incredibly focused, this behavior obviously drives them crazy.

It's kind of like a Barry Manilow concert where, just before the twenty-minute medley of his greatest hits, he says to the audience, "Those of you who have enjoyed the music over the years, you're going to love this medley. Those of you who were dragged here tonight, this medley is going to be agony."

Recently I read the evaluations from my last class and was surprised that many of the participants put down in writing that their favorite part of my class was the stories I tell! I then sat and reflected on my presentation. I realized that more than thirty years in the classroom gives you a lot of stories. And what good is having stories if you don't share them?

Hence, the reason I'm writing this book.

Most people think that when they're going to hear "teacher stories," they're going to hear a bunch of funny anecdotes about weird kids. That is not what this book is about. This is a book of stories of a teacher's life—good, bad, and strange—over an entire career. It's a retelling of things I've lived through and a sharing of things I've learned as a teacher. Some funny, some sad, some informative. But all of it is very personal, and will, I hope, affect the teacher reading this book.

For those of you who are not teachers, maybe it will give you some insight as to what being a teacher really means—a contrast to the negative view of us that is presented by the media. Besides, you, too, may see some aspect of yourself in the book: as a parent or as anyone who deals with kids. Or bureaucracies.

And for those who still ask me, "What's a nice Jewish boy with a Ph.D. doing still teaching in the classroom?" I hope this book will answer the question.

And I hope my mom will finally get off my back about it.

Setting the Context for All of This

I grew up in a suburban public school district in Cleveland, Ohio, and received my teaching degree and credential from The Ohio State University. I moved out to Los Angeles, California, for my graduate work, and earned a Ph.D. in Curriculum and Instruction from the University of Southern California.

My first formal teaching experience was in private education, and by the age of 26 I was the principal of a private school. That lasted one year, after which I went over to the public school system, where they're more sane.

My first teaching experience in public education was eight years in elementary school. I then transferred to a performing arts magnet middle school where I've been for over thirty-five years, teaching musical theater, English, and history.

As a National Board Certified teacher, I regularly present teacher salary point classes and professional development workshops.

And looking back, there's nothing I would have changed in my entire career.

1

How It All Started

I consider myself a "born teacher." I've never wanted to do anything else. Most teachers can remember when they first started teaching. When did I start? Believe it or not, I did my first teaching in sixth grade, when I was twelve years old. It wasn't a formal class, obviously, but it was my first "teaching experience"—and I was hooked.

It was in elementary school. I was really into science and had just discovered how to grow penicillin from moldy bread. (I can still remember the dining room cabinet where I hid the wet, smelly bread in darkness, away from my mother's eyes.) I would then look at the mold under my microscope—for which I already had a fairly large collection of premade slides of bug parts, spores, and other yucky stuff to adults, but fascinating subject matter for a twelve-year-old boy.

My brother was in the first grade at the time, and his class was learning something about science. He wanted me to bring my "experiment" to his class to show his friends. I asked my teacher for permission, which I received (probably just an excuse to get me out of her class that day). My brother's teacher also agreed, but she insisted that I teach a complete science lesson to the students, not just conduct a "show and tell" session. So I did, and it was so successful that I went in there to teach "science" once a week for the next month.

I was hooked.

My first real class actually came only two years later, when I was fourteen. I taught a class at my temple Hebrew school. For anyone who doesn't know what a Hebrew school class is like, it's two hours of subjects that the students often do not care about, taught after their full school day and Sunday morning, and which they are forced to attend, preventing them from playing outside with their friends. To say that the students lack motivation is an understatement.

I was given a class of about fifteen "rejects"—twelve-year-olds who basically got kicked out of their other classes. Somehow the principal thought I could relate to them. So I had this class three times a week for two hours at a shot. I had to make lesson plans, grade their papers, and teach the class. And I got paid for it!

I quickly learned the joy of getting paid for doing what you love! It was a great feeling—still is.

And I've been teaching ever since, with one year off for my junior year of college abroad. So, in reality, I've been formally teaching classes for over forty-five years now!

Sigh.

2

These Ain't the "Good Ole Days"

When I first started teaching in public school, I could brainstorm a lesson driving to school and incorporate it immediately into my teaching. If a student had a rough day, I could give her a hug. I could give a parent my phone number, provide advice when she called, and get a thank-you for my time. Community members regularly expressed their appreciation for what the school and teaching staff meant to their neighborhood. "Testing" was limited to a multiple-choice, standardized test over two or three days in May—and those scores meant little more than subsequent student placement. College graduates enthusiastically went into teaching and looked forward to spending a twenty- to thirty-year career doing what they loved.

Those were the "good ole days."

I have watched things change considerably in education over the past thirty-plus years—unfortunately, not for the better. As a result, it takes more determination than ever to choose to go into the teaching profession, let alone be successful in it. More than once, my wife and I have had to sit down and remind ourselves why we're in this profession—and why we stay.

Since early in this century, there are those in our society who have done their best to destroy public education. Starting with the horrific No Child Left Behind Act (NCLB) in 2002, testing—and, more important, test scores—have become the sole determinant for judging the quality of education. Teacher creativity has been hampered, if not destroyed. Politicians and policymakers have tried to make teachers into robots. I once had a principal, during the time of NCLB, who directed the staff: "If it's not tested, you are not to teach it." Teaching as an art, as a profession, was now on life-support.

As a result of this attitude toward education, we've raised a new generation of young teachers who have no concept of what it is to teach "outside the box." Teachers today are instructed that teaching means following a specific standard, timeline, or established curriculum. In other words, they don't know how to be creative as teachers or to use their personal professional judgment in planning for their students.

I am often asked, as an experienced teacher, how I personally deal with this anti-teacher environment. The answer is that I regularly use the most important teaching tool I have in my classroom: the door.

When my door is shut, I do what I know is right for my students. I'm the professional, and it's my classroom. Ultimately, I'm responsible for what goes on with my students—not an administrator who doesn't know my class, my curricula, or my teaching style. So I teach *my* way, the way my years of experience, training, and education have led me to.

That is the number-one piece of advice I can ever give to a new teacher, and probably the overall theme of this book. As a trained professional educator, do what you know is right for your students.

Overall, parents have also changed considerably over the years. Though it is a generalization, when I first started teaching, our greatest problem with some parents was that they tried to be their child's "friend," rather than the "adult." Then we moved to "helicopter" parents—those parents who hovered over the teacher and school questioning or trying to observe everything that they did.

Unfortunately, we now have a number of parents who act as their child's "agent.[1]" These are parents who *demand* special treatment for their child—even at the expense of the other students in the room. And it's pervasive: I've heard numerous reports of parents going in to see their child's *university professor* to discuss grades! The ultimate example was the report of the parent of a first-year teacher who went in to see the principal when her child got a poor evaluation.

So, how do I deal with this phenomenon? I use the same techniques I talk about in "Parents Are Your Greatest Allies" (Chapter 22 in this book). I sell my program to the vast majority of the parents. The "challenging" parents? Those I judge on a case-by-case basis. I ask myself, is this parent someone I can work with, someone who will be somewhat reasonable? Or is it a parent for whom I have no hope—that nothing I do will make this parent happy. If it's the former, I use whatever logic and strategies I can to make the parent into a partner. If it's the latter, I face the limits of my influence and cut my losses. It may be that I only correspond with the problem parent in writing; it may be that I only meet with this parent with an administrator present; it may be that I demand the child be transferred from my class. Each case is different, but I will do whatever I need for the sake of my professionalism and sanity. And no matter what, I keep a log of all contact and correspondence with a problem parent. Keeping a detailed log can be critical later on, if the parent ever "reports" you and you're called in to defend yourself.

---

1 See S. Mandel. (2007). *The parent-teacher partnership: How to work together for student achievement.* Chicago: Zephyr Press.

Ultimately, teachers need to accept the fact that students have also changed considerably over the years. In this age of instant gratification with social media and "on-demand" entertainment, I have found that a good number of kids today simply don't care anymore about standard school opportunities. They'd rather play video games or hang with their friends in person or, most often, on social media. High schools in my area have been cancelling proms and other dances for lack of interest. One local high school made it mandatory for any student in organized fall sports to attend the Homecoming Dance. That was the only way they could drum up participation.

This unfortunate phenomenon has even affected my performing arts group. My Pacoima Singers are usually the most popular magnet production group for which students audition. We perform around the country and are known for our quality performances. A couple of years ago, I had *seven* (out of seventeen) eighth graders quit in the middle of the year! I hadn't had seven students quit in my previous twenty-plus years with the group. Their reasons? Not that they were upset with me; not that they didn't get solos. They quit because they didn't want to attend afterschool rehearsals—they wanted to hang out with their friends. They had absolutely no desire to fulfill their commitments or put in any significant effort. Even worse, their parents allowed them to renege on their personal commitment to the group. What kind of "life lessons" are these parents teaching their children? One has to wonder what they will be like in the real working world one day.

How do I deal with this phenomenon? I keep my standards high. I don't lower them to meet these students' expectations in the hope of appeasing them so that they'll stay in the group. And I concentrate on the other twenty-seven kids in the group who *do* want to be there, who do want the positive experiences I can provide. I may not affect as many kids as I used to, but I affect many kids as much as I ever have.

Still, through it all—even with the changes in society, parents, and students—there's nothing I would want to do as much as work with kids, educate them, watch them grow and develop. As times change, I obviously have to adapt to those changes. But the core reasons why I have devoted my life to teaching are still there.

That's what makes it still worthwhile, and it's my message to you, the reader. Be the professional, do what you know is right as a teacher, and adapt to the changes you'll experience over the years.

And that's why I'll keep going on this job as long as I'm physically able to do it—or until that coffin (my personal retirement plan—see Chapter 19) in the corner of my room gets put to use.

Now that you've learned how I started this long teaching career and have been brought up to date with what teaching is like in today's times, it's time for me to fill you in on all of the middle years—the experiences, ideas, thoughts, and fun I've had as a public school teacher for the last thirty-some years.

Read on!

3

How My Students Saved My Life and the School Year

About nine years ago I was diagnosed with cancer—I was actually rushed to the hospital the night before school began in September. Luckily, I had a very rare form of lymphoma—only a thousand men in their 50s get it each year, and it's 100% curable. As my doctors said: If I were going to get sick, this was what I should have.

After a week, when they finally figured out the exact diagnosis and treatment, I went back to school. I eventually had this new chemo that comes in a pump with a pic-line into your arm that you wear in a fanny-pack for one week. It doesn't make you sick; you don't lose your hair; and you can work while you wear it.

Unfortunately, the chemo also kills your immune system to a point where you are left quite susceptible to infection.

My primary job at school is Director of the Pacoima Singers—a production class in our performing arts magnet that performs widely. Now, having our first major Singers show of the year in mid-October, I insisted on going back to work for rehearsals while trying to avoid any significant contact with the kids. Not my smartest decision.

My doctor always likes to point out that doctors and teachers are the worst patients. If I had been a lawyer, accountant, engineer, etc., I would have had no problem taking the two or three months off I should have taken. No—doctors and teachers feel a need to get back to work as soon as possible.

Two weeks later, I was in the hospital, literally dying from an infection. I spent two-and-a-half weeks there before I came home. The nurses and doctors said it was nothing short of amazing, since someone as sick as I was should have been in the hospital for two or three months.

I believe that my students, and obviously God, pulled me through it.

It's amazing, when you're alone at night in a hospital bed, the things you pray for and the deals you make with God for getting you through it. I know it sounds corny, and I always believed that it was "TV-ish." But when you go through it yourself, you find it's very true.

I found myself not bargaining that I didn't want to die. Rather, my primary argument was that I had to recover: I had too much good left to do in the world for my students. I still had many young lives to mold. Obviously God agreed, because here I am today.

After going home from the hospital, I was able to return to school in two weeks, right after Thanksgiving break, for the last three weeks of school—and for our Winter Show.

This experience was also an example of what life can be like for a teacher when you have a great principal. Many principals would say that you cannot come back to work until you are 100% better and able to completely fulfill your duties. My wonderful principal gave me permission to come and go as I needed. I could come in late if need be, or leave early if I had to, all depending on how I was feeling. My classes were always covered.

All in all, from September through December, I missed a total of eight weeks of school (a testament to the wisdom of saving up your sick days).

What about my singing group?

Luckily, we had a one-day workshop the last week of vacation in which the students were provided with most of their music for the fall semester. Additional material was given to them when I was in class, along with basic directions on how choreography should be designed and how the songs should be blocked. In my absence over the eight weeks, my student officers (assistant directors and choreographers) literally ran the group and every class period while the substitute teacher—who was not a music teacher—watched and supported them. The students created the choreography, taught it, and ran all of the rehearsals—all the more remarkable when you remember that they were 12, 13, and 14 year-olds.

During Winter Show, I literally sat and watched my kids perform. I found myself leaning over to my wife on more than one occasion, saying, "I've never seen that before!" It was truly one of the proudest moments I've had as a teacher—that I was able to get my kids to a point where they could work so incredibly independently and cooperatively, that everything could function even without me there for an extended period of time.

The only significant problem we encountered occurred in January, when I was completely recovered and back to work full-time. My officers and I had a number of "battles" over the direction of the group.

They didn't want to give up the power they had enjoyed during fall semester.

4

Let the Kids Know You Can Have Fun, Too

This chapter is about having fun as a teacher. It's one of the most important qualities you can develop—and it's directly tied to your classroom success.

Over my twenty-five-plus years at my school, I've acquired a reputation as perhaps the hardest, strictest teacher in the school. I probably give more D's and F's than any teacher, and I continuously hold the students accountable for their behavior. (I'm proud that my sixth-grade students often refer to me playfully as "evil" or "mean and rotten.") But a strange thing often happens in parent conferences—no matter how bad a student's grades have been, or how much trouble he's been in, when the parent asks the student if he wants to switch from my class to an easier one, the response is always an emphatic "NO!"

I can't get rid of these kids. [*Sarcastic smile.*]

What's the secret? My students have too much fun in my class—plain and simple. As tough as I am, as much work as I give them, I keep it fun. And that starts with me having fun in front of them.

Basically, I love my job, and I show it. I've always been one of the only ones among my friends who professed to love their jobs. I can't understand how anyone can spend eight hours a day at a job they don't like.

There are numerous situations that simply lend themselves to "teacher comedy." Spelling tests are always a great opportunity for humor. For example, the month before report cards come out, each spelling sentence I create is about what's going to happen to them when their parents see their report cards. And it's usually not pretty.

In class, we regularly joke around, and I'm quite obnoxious (within reason, of course [*again, sarcastic smile*]). In fact, I generally don't yell or get upset. Instead, I get sarcastic, which the students sometimes appreciate more. Or, as one student once admitted: it's not all the referrals I give out that bother him, it's the fact that I'm always smiling when I do it! More on that strategy later, when I talk about discipline.

Whereas I never recommend to new teachers that sarcasm be used as a normal classroom management technique—it's a refined skill literally developed over decades—teachers can still start showing their "fun" side in other ways. Humor, whenever appropriate, should be regularly used by the teacher—appropriate to the grade level, of course.

The most important way to demonstrate your "fun" side is by always participating in school activities. Special dress-up days, special sports activities, special programs—the more you as a teacher participate, the more the students can see how much fun you can be. They see your human side.

Even how you set up your room affects the way in which the students view you. My room is decorated in Cleveland Browns and Ohio State memorabilia, and we talk some football every Monday during the autumn season. And, of course, I always wear a special Browns shirt to school on Mondays after a win. (Unfortunately, it hasn't gotten a lot of wear in recent years.)

However, Halloween probably provides the best opportunity to show the students that you can have fun. To this day, I cannot understand teachers who hate Halloween and refuse to dress up, even minimally. The students notice immediately who's "cool" and participating, and who's not. And it often affects their perspective of that teacher.

Then again, I don't advocate for teachers to go to the extreme that I do. I have a reputation for usually dressing like a woman on Halloween. Literally, dozens of students (and staff) quiz me for a week before the holiday as to what I'm going to wear. My singing group always dresses together as a "theme" (i.e., Disney, TV characters, or superheroes), and I join in. Over the years I've appeared at school dressed as Tinker Bell, Mary Poppins, Elsa, Lucy, or Annie, and they're still talking about the day I came in as Wonder Woman.

Showing that you can have fun, or being "human" in the students' eyes, is critical to earning their respect and cooperation. It helps the students stop doing your work because they *have* to, and begin doing it because they want to please or connect with you. But as I stated at the beginning of this chapter, being a "fun" teacher does not take away from being a "strict" or "hard" teacher.

However, being "human" in the students' eyes is not equivalent to being their "friend." There is a line that I never let them cross—the one that separates me as their teacher from them as my students. There is a certain level of respect that I demand. For example, I never let them call me by my last name only, as they do with their friends. I tell them, "You can call me Dr. Mandel, Mr. Mandel, sir, your honor, my lord, my liege, or anything like that—but you can't just call me Mandel." It's a fundamental line of respect.

It's your basic personality and how you relate to your students that determine more than anything how they will respect you and relate to you. I once had a principal whose pet peeve was insisting that the teachers dress in a "professional" manner. Even though he could not enforce it, he wanted male teachers to dress in ties, and women in dresses or skirts. He insisted that dressing that way would increase student respect toward the teacher. We laughed. It just so happened that particular year that some of the least respected teachers on staff all wore ties, whereas four of the most respected teachers regularly came in t-shirts and jeans. (Of course, some highly respected teachers wore ties, too—I'm not labeling all tie-wearers!). I kept trying to convince the principal that it's not the clothes that get kids' respect—it's how you treat those kids, respect them, and let them know that you're human and can have fun, too.

Then again, having fun with the students can sometimes backfire, as I have discovered more than once. The "personality" of my singing group varies from year to year. One year, the boys in my group were very "macho." They played basketball every lunch period, and we continually talked sports together. During one of our Washington, D.C., trips, we were all fooling around on the grass near the Washington Monument, where we were celebrating our performance that day, and one of the boys tackled me from behind. It was not meant maliciously, but as fun horseplay. I went to the ground on my shoulder and immediately knew it was injured. The boys were all laughing hysterically that they had "gotten me." Obviously, I could not just allow this assault on the Alpha Male to go "unpunished," so although I was in significant pain, I got up, chased the perpetrator, and tackled him back. (Obviously, this was back in the day when teachers and students could physically interact in harmless horseplay.) Of course it was all in fun—and the boys actually felt bad when the bus had to drop me off later at the hospital to tend to my separated shoulder. But I was content. The group's "Alpha Male" had held his position (though to this day my wife hasn't let me live down this incident).

No matter how "hard" a teacher you are, no matter how difficult your course is, let the students know that you can have fun, too. It lets them see you're human, and their respect for you will grow.

5

Kids Don't Care How Much You Know as Long as They Know You Care

One of my favorite educational quotes comes from former president of the NEA (National Education Association) Reg Weaver: "Kids don't care how much you know, as long as they know you care." And when you show them that you know how to have fun, that you can laugh and have a good time with them, it's one of the best ways to show them that you care. But I need to elaborate more on what this philosophy means to the everyday teacher.

Once upon a time, many, many years ago (even before I started teaching), teachers were professionals who taught lessons; students went home to a stable traditional nuclear family; and parents and community supported the educational professionals of the neighborhood public school. Wow, have things changed! Now teachers not only teach, but we have become pseudo-parents, counselors, psychologists, social workers, medical personnel, and who knows how many other things. I'm not saying that this is right or wrong—I'm just saying that it is the state of our educational profession today.

I believe that we need to take a holistic view of the student—that in order to reach the child, we need to consider all aspects of the student's life. Many years ago the government began to feed kids at school in the belief that a hungry child cannot learn. In today's society, this concept must be expanded to embrace the concept that a troubled child will not learn.

This does not mean that we as teachers are expected to solve the student's outside problems. We are not equipped to do that. However, sometimes the best thing that a student needs to know is that you care. And nowadays, we are too often the only ones who really care.

We have the opportunity to demonstrate to our students every day that we truly care. The following are a number of practices that I regularly implement when dealing with my students with problems.

Establishing a relationship. I always call my new sixth-grade students at home the weekend before school. I welcome them and their parents and ask if they have any questions. It makes them feel more secure and less stressed about beginning their middle-school experience.

Establishing contact. I regularly give my parents my phone number and e-mail. And no—in over thirty years of doing this, it has been abused only once. I have discovered over the years that the majority of problems I've had with parents are related to communication issues. Through a phone call or e-mail, problems can often be taken care of immediately—before they fester and get worse. At the same time, I have limits. I inform parents that it's inappropriate to call me or e-mail me for homework help or because their child forgot the assignment. And they can't call me during Browns games.

I also do not "friend" any student or parent on social media. That's where I draw a line. There's too much of my personal life to which I do not want them to have access. I will only "friend" parents, or see them socially, after the student leaves my class and graduates from middle school. I will only "friend" former students on Facebook after they graduate from high school.

Divorce. Many of our students' parents are either going through a divorce during the school year or have already been divorced. I'm going to address these two situations separately.

Students whose parent are going through a divorce—regardless of their age—are deeply affected. I always let them know that they can talk to me at any time if they feel the need, or I can arrange for them to talk to a counselor at the school. This is especially important when the divorce is nastier than usual, or the parents are using the children as pawns. This can lead, at times, to very traumatized students. If the students are missing work some days (for those students who rarely miss work), I will often give them a "break" and allow them more time.

More than anything else, these students somotimes just need a hug. Yes, I know with today's child-abuse mania we as teachers are not supposed to hug kids. But if one of my kids is crying because of trauma at home, I'm going to let them hug me. (However, I always take a couple common-sense precautions—I make sure it's done in public, and I let the child initiate the hug, with my hands out, a couple of inches away, not actually touching the student.) But sometimes nothing lets a child know you care more than a hug when he or she is traumatized.

For students who live with divorced parents, the problems may not be as traumatic, but they're still serious. First, for those students who live in a shared custody arrangement, I make sure they get two sets of textbooks. This way they don't have to deal with leaving books at one of their homes when they are at the other. Second, I insist that both parents come to conferences (preferably together), and I work with them to get them on the same page and to reduce the chance of the student playing one parent off the other.

Recognizing that they're kids. This point is especially true for kids between the ages of 11 and 15, when their hormones and peer relationships affect their decisions more than anything else. Sometimes you need to show some compassion and give them a break when they do something "dumb" (for lack of a better descriptor). For example, in the case of sixth graders, if during spring semester two students are having a problem, the first question I usually ask is "Who broke up with whom?" (Very often that is the cause of the problem.) I then tell them to knock it off, and the matter is usually dropped. But very often the root of the problem is peer-group difficulty. Being understanding at these times goes a long way with the student.

On a more serious note, sometimes students get into a rut and fall behind to the point where it's virtually impossible for them to catch up. This is especially true for students entering a new school (i.e., sixth or ninth graders) or have experienced some trauma recently (e.g., a divorce). Even if they turn the corner and want to practice better work habits, they cannot realistically catch up. What I will sometimes do, during a parent conference, is offer to throw out all of the previous poor grades and pretend that the student is "brand new" to the school. This "deal" comes with the understanding that this will only go into effect if all work is now turned in, at an appropriate level of quality. I have found that, given this chance to start fresh, about 50% of the time the student turns himself around and does A/B work. In the other 50% of cases, the student does not change the behavior and ends up with the same grade he or she would have gotten had I not thrown out the previous grades. Either way, I recognize that things happen, that they are kids, and I provide them with an opportunity to succeed.

You're your students' advocate. Nothing lets your students know you care more than being their advocate. Whether it's with other students or teachers, my kids know that they can come to me if they feel they have been treated unfairly, and I will investigate and advocate for them. At the same time, that doesn't mean that I will automatically take their side. If they prove to be on the wrong side of an issue, I will wholeheartedly support any consequences they may suffer. But either way, they know that I care enough to take the time to listen to them and follow through with an investigation as to the merits of their situation.

When your students know you care, they are so much more apt to listen to you, do what you request of them academically, and get more out of your classroom experience. More important, you are helping them become better people, and you truly become a significant part of their overall development, not just their intellectual development.

6

If I Don't Talk about Discipline, You Won't Read This Book

Students in the teacher education department at my alma mater take six quarters of classes over a two-year period, culminating in a B.S. Ed. degree and state teacher certification. This allows the students to take many more education courses than most Schools of Education offer. As a result, at the beginning their programs, all education students must take an Intro to Education course that provides the very basics of teaching. It's a course I'll never forget, but not for the reasons you may think.

I had a wonderful relationship with my professor in this class, since I was already a fairly experienced teacher when I attended. Whereas not one of the other students had ever taught children, I began my career as a paid teacher for afternoon religious schools at age fourteen. (As I described earlier, this was one of the my hardest gigs, as the kids really did not want to attend. And yes—that just reminded me that I've been teaching children in some form for about fifty years!).

By the time I enrolled in this Introduction to Teaching class, I already had seven years of teaching experience. As a result, we were able to discuss more advanced issues about teaching methodologies and curricula—in-depth issues that would normally not be presented to students in such an introductory class. It was a marvelous experience.

The professor and I enjoyed a good laugh together about certain facets of the intro class, especially on the day that the topic was DISCIPLINE—the topic about which every new teacher seems to be obsessed.

On "Discipline Day," as we called it, the professor lectured about discipline in very general terms, about how it should be adapted, modified to fit the situation, and other, similar aspects. She tried to stress that good classroom management alleviates most disciplinary problems, but the students would not accept this philosophy. They seemed to believe that "discipline" was a subject unto itself, one that needed to be studied. As a result, the participants in the class kept pressing her on specifics, but she wouldn't go there. As the class went on, the questions on particulars became more frequent, and the students became more frustrated with her "non-answers." Finally, they pinned her down on how she once handled a particular event, and as she answered, the pens went flying. Every student in that room desperately tried to write down every word she said.

That anecdote exemplifies my basic rule about "discipline" that I've developed from my long career in teaching:[1]

There is no one disciplinary rule that a teacher can always use.

As a teacher, I've discovered that what works at 9 A.M. is different from what works at 2 P.M. What works on Monday differs from what works on Friday. What works on a sunny, hot day varies from what works on a rainy or windy day. And I wholeheartedly maintain that an elementary school teacher can tell it's a full moon without bothering to look outside.

1 For an extensive discussion about the ten aspects of classroom discipline, see Mandel (2009) in the "References" section of this book.

My advice to teachers about formulating a discipline policy is based on what I wrote in the previous chapter. If the kids know you care, if they know you respect them, your discipline problems will be significantly reduced. I believe it really is that simple. Students today are not like students were even ten years ago. I don't know if it's the proliferation of social media, or smartphones in every pocket. Maybe it's a result of school policies that no longer allow negative repercussions, such as suspension for "willful defiance." But I do know that kids today no longer fear teachers, deans, or even administrators as authority figures. Today, if you yell at a middle or high school student, the reaction is not a cowering in fear—rather, it may well result in being cursed out by the student, knowing that there would be little, if anything, the adult could do about it. Unfortunately, that's the state of our schools today. However, that doesn't mean teachers are doomed to this fate. Instead, it means we have to change our tactics. Respect, not power, needs to be the basis of a good discipline policy. If you talk to them in a respectful way, students will respond in kind.

Two stories illustrate how students react when they feel that you respect them. The first happened many years ago when I was teaching elementary school. I was in a set of bungalows—five rooms connected together by interior doors. We had a break-in one night, and we knew it was an "inside job." In one room, that of a teacher who was known to be "mean" and disrespectful to students, the room was trashed so badly that the intruders even defecated in her aquarium. The other three rooms had varying levels of destruction, depending on the other teachers' reputations. My room? They played computer games and played with my classroom pet rat. I felt a bit guilty, but I actually felt complimented that I was respected that much!

Teachers need to understand that students who feel disrespected will get them back, not necessarily to the extremes of the above example. But they will do it in other, subtle and not-so-subtle ways, ranging from disrupting your class, to a personal work stoppage, to something more extreme like textbook or desk graffiti. This is especially true in today's society, as stated earlier.

The second example occurred in the back bungalows of my middle school, where the eighth graders are mostly housed. Between periods, I was walking by and saw a couple of eighth graders play-fighting and kicking each other. I told them to cut it out, and one of them (the largest one) started to come my way, yelling a challenge at me. One of his friends immediately stopped him, saying, "Hey man, leave him alone. He's cool." Now, I had no idea who either of these kids were, but I smiled and nodded to them.

Now, not everything is perfect in my classroom—not by far—and I don't want to give anyone that impression. Occasionally I need to discipline a student. However, there are certain principles that I try to exemplify. First, I always strive to correct the *behavior*, not the *student*. For example, I rarely kick a student out of my class—often that is what the student wants, and the lesson is missed, thereby putting the offender behind the following day. If I need to remove the child from my classroom, I'll send the student and the day's work to another classroom to sit and work. If the offense isn't bad enough to warrant removal, I'll put the child in a doorway or corner of the room, facing me, in a form of "time out." I let the student know that as soon as he feels he can change his behavior and rejoin the classroom and lesson, he's welcome to get up and go back to his seat. If he's in the "time out" and raises his hand to participate, I always call on him. I never put a time limit on the student by, for example, saying that he needs to "sit there for a half hour." Rather, as soon as the negative behavior is extinguished, the student can rejoin the class. It may take only five minutes, or it may take an hour. *The behavior is always the issue, not the student personally.*

One of my favorite stories involves one of my first years at my school. I was teaching an eighth-grade history class, and I had the "class clown" on my roster. He was small, with a very slight build. He was the kind of kid that one would expect would be picked on in an eighth-grade class. What saved him socially was that he would act up and get himself kicked out of class virtually every day. Well, the second day in class, as I was beginning my lesson, he made a really loud, obnoxious comment to me that cracked up the class. Not even waiting for me to react, he started to put his backpack together, expecting to be kicked out of class. Instead, I made a sarcastic comment back at him. He stopped—there was silence in the room, no one knew what was happening. He looked at me, and made another crack at me. I smiled and made a sarcastic comment back at him—and the class started to giggle. Embarrassed, the boy said something to me, and I came right back. Now the class was starting to outwardly laugh, and the boy was getting really frustrated. He made one more attempt to rile me, and I came back, one, two, three obnoxious cracks before he could react. By this time, the class was rolling in laughter, and he was speechless. I walked up to him and said, "I'm better at this than you. Are you done now?" He nodded, and sat down. I never had another problem with him all year.

Two codas to this story: First, about six months later, the boy made a sarcastic crack, immediately caught himself, and apologized profusely. I laughed and told him it was okay, that his line was actually funny. Second, toward the end of the year, his other teachers approached me and invited me to a meeting with his parents, because they were finally going to "get him." I informed them that they didn't really want me at that meeting, because I was having no problem with him, and that he was getting a "B" in my class. The teachers were upset ... at me! They felt that my giving him a good grade was going to make them look bad!

Now, I do not recommend that you take this type of approach—using extreme sarcasm—when dealing with certain problematic students. It's taken me many years to know what I can and cannot say, and to develop my reputation. And it's also doubtful that in today's society I would use this extreme approach again. But my point is that it's important to understand where kids are coming from, their background, and—especially in secondary levels—their social standing. Starting around fifth grade and continuing through high school, the students' social group is much more important to them than any teacher relationship. If you come across as a threat to their "rep," they will act out in a form of "social self-defense"—even if they know that there will be negative consequences to their behavior! Understanding and respecting a teenager's social standing is key to a positive classroom relationship. In their eyes, their social standing is more important than anything you can do to them.

I will never forget the year that I taught eighth-grade English. I had a major "gang-banger" in the class. He was about 250 pounds, shaved head, gang-type clothes. He had a perpetual scowl on his face—never smiled, never participated verbally in class. He was the kind of student most teachers would fear. Throughout the year, whenever I handed back one of his tests or assignments, I'd also have a scowl on my face—a sort of "of course you did lousy again" type of expression, and toss the paper upside down on his desk. He'd look at it with disgust, and shove it into his back pocket. What nobody knew was that the paper almost always had an "A" grade on it. I played the game with him to protect his "rep," and he responded positively. He never missed my class, and never displayed negative behaviors. And at the end of the year, everyone was shocked when I nominated him for the Top English Student award—which he accepted with pride!

Besides respect, the other aspect of discipline that I believe is crucial is striving to be fair. Being fair is critical to gaining the respect of your students. For example, when a student comes to me to complain that another student hit him, the first question I ask is, "What did you do to cause him to hit you?" We discuss how it is extremely rare for a student to hit another out of the blue. Inevitably, the "hittee" admits to doing something to provoke the "hitter." I point out the fact that if he didn't provoke the "hitter," he would not have reacted as he did. Thereafter, if a negative consequence was to be issued, both parties would get it—the "provoker" and the "provokee." The students immediately witness that I am doing my best to be fair—and that goes a long way with them.

At the same time, I demand respect from my students. They can talk to me as an adult, and they can disagree with me vehemently—but it needs to be done respectfully. No raising of the voice; no profanity. And as I mentioned earlier, my personal peeve—which I do not allow—is for them to call me by my last name only. That, in my view, is a major sign of disrespect. I tell the students they can call me "Dr. Mandel," "Mr. Mandel," "Your Honor," "My Liege," "Oh Great One"—anything but just "Mandel."

In closing this chapter on discipline, I want to share two ideas that I've learned over the years, insights that help me more than anything else to keep a measure of sane control in my classrooms. The first is learning how to ignore. Minor incidents that don't disrupt the class and do little more than annoy you should be ignored. Otherwise you'll become increasingly frustrated throughout the day—especially when the students figure out your annoyance level. This practice also helps you gain respect from the students, as they observe that you don't react negatively to every little infraction that they commit.

I practice this all the time at my school. For example, dealing with cell phones on the campus is a continual problem and nuisance. The students are not supposed to have them out during the school day. However, they continually do so during passing periods, break times, or lunch. Theoretically, as teachers, we're supposed to take them away when we see them and bring the phone to the office. Most teachers simply ignore the phones. However, if I pass a student with a phone out, I'll often say, "Wow, it's a good thing I'm so old and my eyesight is so bad and decrepit. If I actually saw that phone out, I'd have to take it." The student smiles and puts it away, getting the message and learning a new vocabulary word at the same time.

The critical second insight that I've learned is never to show negative emotion when disciplining a student. I may be livid with the student's behavior—but I'll never let them see it. If anything, I'll be smiling and laughing as I hand out a negative consequence.

There's actually a logic behind this. Students have limited control over what happens in their lives. However, they know that they can control your emotions. Think about it. As a teacher or a parent, have you ever seen children get in trouble and then argue continuously and vehemently about it? They know they're not going to get out of trouble, and they know that most likely, the more they argue, the worse the punishment is going to be. So why do they do it? Because they know that you're getting increasingly upset—and in their minds, if they're going down, they're going to take you with them! So how do you keep this from happening? Do not show negative emotion—no matter how upset you may be. If they know that they have no effect on you, many of the escalating behaviors will be extinguished.

One of my favorite memories involves a former student saying to me, "It's not all of your referrals that bothered me—it was the fact that you were always smiling when you gave them to me!" I love that comment—I was doing something right.

Ultimately, if I were to be asked what makes a good discipline policy, I would say this: Respect and Fairness. Add those to good classroom management, and everything else connected to discipline will fall into place.

7

Public School Kids Deserve the Same as Private School Kids

My first assignment teaching in Los Angeles was teaching fourth grade at a local private school. The fourth-grade social studies curriculum was based on California history. As a special treat, the students flew up to the state capital for a day, where they visited the capitol building, the Blue Diamond Almond Factory, the Transportation Museum, and more. It was a great day. They did minimal fundraising, and their parents paid for the bulk of the trip.

Fast forward six years to my first teaching assignment with the Los Angeles Unified School District (LAUSD), teaching fourth grade in a nice, middle-class neighborhood in the Valley. I spoke at length with my principal about how the private school where I had previously taught had taken this one-day trip to Sacramento, and that it was a crime that public school kids couldn't have the same opportunity.

She agreed, and with her permission, we decided to try to raise the money for a similar trip with my students—since, unlike in private schools, we could not charge the parents for a trip during the school day. We had weekly bake sale fundraisers. We conducted a California Trivia-Thon, where the students learned trivia about the state and solicited "sponsors" who would donate a certain amount for every question the students got right. Eventually, we raised the money and were able to give our public school students the same experience students had in private school, without their parents paying for the experience.

After a couple of years of this successful one-day trip, we moved it up a notch and took a sixth-grade trip to Washington, D.C. That's when I developed the fundamental fundraising philosophy that I later used for my Pacoima Singers trips—everyone goes or nobody goes.

To this day—and it's been over twenty trips around the country for my Pacoima Singers—not one student has ever been left behind for financial reasons. We've traveled and performed in Washington, D.C., every other year. In alternate years, we've performed in Vancouver (Canada), Seattle, Chicago, and at the Rock and Roll Hall of Fame in Cleveland. The way the trip is financed is as follows: Parents donate as much as they can, and we fundraise the rest. Total cost for the class for each trip is normally between $35,000 and $45,000. I have some parents who can afford the entire amount, and I have some parents who work as day laborers and give me a $20 bill each month. I'm the only one who knows how much each person contributes. We get sponsors and hold fundraisers for the rest. (Alas, we're no longer allowed to hold bake sales or pizza sales.)

For about twenty years now, even though my school is in a low socioeconomic immigrant neighborhood, not one student has ever been left behind from this once-in-a-lifetime trip because they could not afford the cost. It's one of the things I'm most proud of in my career.

And it all started back in my first public school elementary teaching position, when I insisted that public school kids should have the same opportunities as private school kids!

Okay—now an embarrassing side-story as to why you never take anything for granted, and always check the details: When we went on the Sacramento trip from the private school, we flew out of Burbank Airport, a medium-sized airport in the Valley. (Los Angeles International [LAX] was twice as far away in the city, with lots of rush-hour traffic.) For my trip with the public school, I used the same travel agent as the private school had used. I assumed that everything would be identical, and even though the ticket said "Departing from Los Angeles," I thought that they were referring to the city, and that Burbank Airport was implied.

(People in Los Angeles reading this story are already laughing because they know what's coming next.)

We arrived at Burbank Airport early in the morning with a busload of fourth graders, my principal (who was accompanying us), and *her* boss, who had a fourth-grade son at another school and thought this would be a great opportunity for him.

When I got to the counter—only an hour before the flight—the agent looked at me in horror and proceeded to tell me that we were at the wrong airport, that we were flying out of LAX (Los Angeles International Airport—the "Los Angeles" on the ticket). We now had one hour to go eighteen miles across the city, in a school bus, through horrible rush-hour traffic, to get to LAX. (At this time of day, traveling from Burbank to west Los Angeles would normally take 1½ to 2 hours by car.)

I have never been more appreciative of a bus driver than I was that day. He took us through every back route possible through the entire city of Los Angeles and got us there in less than an hour. As we rushed to the airport, my principal and I were discussing alternate career opportunities that we might need, especially since a district official was with us on this disaster.

Luckily, the flight officials at Burbank called their counterparts at LAX, and they held the plane as 50+ fourth-graders ran through the terminal to get on board. Thankfully, this was years before post-9/11 TSA security!

We made it, the trip was amazing, and a tradition of taking "public school kids" on trips was born. And my principal and I kept our jobs.

8

Have Heroes

In today's world, motivation for success is very different for our students than it was for us, in so many ways. I believe a lot of it begins with a total lack of realistic heroes in our society nowadays.

When we grew up (those of us over 50 or so), heroes abounded. We had political heroes—John F. Kennedy, Robert F. Kennedy; we had societal heroes—Martin Luther King, Jr., Cesar Chavez; we had heroes of courage—NASA astronauts; we had real-life TV heroes—Jacques Cousteau; we had sports heroes—athletes who spent their entire careers with a team before free agency transformed them into mercenaries. And presidents were revered and considered perfect role-models for an American child. When was the last time you heard a child told, "You can grow up to be president"?

So what's happened to all of our heroes?

Political heroes? The quality has diminished over the past few decades. Rarely do you see politicians stand up for a true system of beliefs. And if they do, they are often deemed "non-electable." How many parents today—even if they support a president politically—would want their child to grow up "just like him (the president)"? (And I'm referring to the years before Obama.)

Societal heroes? I haven't seen one in a long time. Can't even conjure up a reason—but what societal figure have we had for our students to look up to in recent years?

Heroes of courage? Name the last NASA astronaut or space flight. Revolutionary inventors such as Bill Gates and Steve Jobs are known more for their corporate skills than past innovative skills.

Sports heroes? Do we have to go there? Since free agency, it is almost unheard of for a player to show extended loyalty to a team. And the superstars are usually more interested in their corporate images. I'll never forget Michael Jordan's comment on why he won't take a position to establish himself as an African American role model: "Republicans buy tennis shoes, too" (or something to that effect).

And presidents? Presidents, and the presidency, were revered until a cultural event that occurred in 1975. No, it wasn't Nixon. He was personally disgraced, not the presidency itself. But until 1975, it was rather rare to hear comedians make fun of the current president.

What was it that caused us to no longer revere the presidency? It was Chevy Chase and *Saturday Night Live*.

Until Chevy Chase frequently portrayed President Ford as a bumbling klutz, TV did not regularly make fun of the presidency. After this portrayal on one of the most popular TV shows of the time, societal respect for the position changed. In fact, I remember a study that I heard of years ago regarding Johnny Carson's monologue (sorry, I don't have a citation). It was discovered that in 1975, when *Saturday Night Live* debuted, Carson averaged about 22 jokes about the president *a month*. Ten years later, he was averaging 22 jokes *a night* about the president. And things haven't changed since.

(For those of you saying "Johnny who?"—sigh—he was the long-time host of *The Tonight Show* before Jay Leno, who was a long-time host before Jimmy Fallon.)

So, what is the point of this discussion? We as teachers need to promote heroes with our students. Who are *your* heroes? Share them. One of mine is John Jacobson, the Founder and Executive Director of the America Sings! Festival. (You read my description of him in the Dedication to this book.)

Another one is LeBron James, who has never been in trouble, never associated with drugs or legal issues, married his high school sweetheart, and after he left to win a championship in Miami, he "came back home" to Cleveland to win a championship and raise his kids in his hometown. In addition, even though he moved on to Los Angeles after achieving his goal, he continues to operate the LeBron James Family Foundation in Ohio, an organization dedicated to giving millions to the community and neighborhood kids. He even opened a state-of-the-art community public school for disadvantaged youth in his hometown. That's a modern-day sports hero.

I try to share my personal heroes with my students. I will often talk to them about former teachers and everyday people whom I've met and who have made an impression on me. For example, one year I taught English to immigrant adults at night. I have never admired a group of people so much. Here they were, after working 8–10 hours a day, often at difficult manual labor, with families at home—and they still took the time and effort to come and learn English.

I share with my students the charitable work done by Bruce Springsteen and the late Harry Chapin. In every one of their concerts, they stopped the music and personally promoted a local charity.

I still talk about the parent, a day laborer making less than minimum wage, who made sure that he contributed a $20 bill every month for his daughter's trip with my singing group.

Why is it important to promote heroes among our students? Because it gives them someone to look up to, someone to emulate, a goal of behavior for which to strive. It provides them with the inspiration to become more than they currently are. It goes beyond preparing our students for the annual test or a college education. It goes directly toward making them better human beings.

This is one of the reasons I so admire the Character Counts program of Michael Josephson. He promotes role models and high moral character among all people, using his Six Pillars of Character:[1] Trustworthiness, Fairness, Respect, Caring, Responsibility, and Citizenship. (Check out his website at https://charactercounts.org.)

Ultimately, I try to instill in my students the concept that they have a personal responsibility to make the world a little better when they leave than it was when they got here. How do they do that? By emulating the behavior of their heroes.

We know how important it is to teach our students the basics for becoming a productive person as an adult. But we also need to teach them how to be better human beings. I know it's not tested, and it's not in our textbooks, but we need to do it in the discussions that we have, and instill in them the importance of having heroes to look up to. It's one of the most essential lessons we as teachers can provide.

And it's what good, career teachers do.

---

1 Josephson, M. (2002). *Making ethical decisions.* Los Angeles: Josephson Institute of Ethics.

9

Get Rid of Your Ego

I had to get over my professional ego years ago with my doctorate advisor at USC. She was wonderful and realistic. I'll never forget my first dissertation proposal. I worked on it for months and was really proud of it when I handed it to her. I'll never forget what she wrote on it when she handed it back. Sprawled across the front page, in red ink, it said:

THIS IS CRAP
DO IT OVER

My ego flew out the window right there.

Okay—I know this might be a seemingly hypocritical title for a chapter in a book that may seem like the ultimate teacher ego trip. And everyone needs a healthy ego to be successful. However, the "ego" that I'm talking about refers to the one in the classroom—the ego that makes a teacher think she's always right and keeps her from ever admitting to a bad lesson or a bad decision.

I believe that if you never have a lesson that fails, you've never tried anything new. None of us has ever been a "perfect" teacher—none of us has lessons that *always* work.

Unfortunately, too often your ego gets in the way of that realization.

As a teacher, we need to keep our egos in check, especially when working with kids. (I'm not talking about humorous situations such as when I have the word "because" on my spelling test, and I use the sentence: "To a teacher or parent, 'because' is a complete sentence." It's a teacher/parent ego/power thing.)

You should never be afraid to admit you're wrong to your students. Sometimes you are. Sometimes you react based on incomplete information; sometimes you react because you're in a really bad mood. Either way, when you determine that you're wrong, it's important for your credibility in the students' eyes to admit it. This is especially true when the *students* know you're wrong.

Unfortunately, I've seen too many teachers over the years be stubborn and never admit to being wrong in front of their students. Either they felt it was a sign of weakness or their ego was too big. They would rather "stick to their story" than admit anything. And just as unfortunate, their students were normally the ones who had little respect for their teacher.

I've always gone by the concept that depending on the size of my personal screw-up, that's the size of my *mea culpa*. It may be offered privately to a student, or it may be a public apology in front of the class. More than once, it's resulted in my purchasing donuts for the class. But the result is that my students realize that I'm human, and that I take personal responsibility for my mistakes.

It's this type of modeling behavior that teaches our students the adult life behaviors that we want them to learn. More important, it leads to the type of respect that we as teachers usually only dream of getting from our students.

10

Support Your Home Team

The first thing you see when you walk into my classroom is a huge Cleveland Browns flag on the wall. You will see numerous Browns, Indians, Cavs, and Ohio State Buckeyes memorabilia around my classroom—and no, I don't give equal time to other teams. I'm from Cleveland, Ohio, and am a die-hard Cleveland sports fan.

And that's not an easy thing to admit. During the football season, I often wear a Browns shirt that says "Just One Before I Die" (referring to a championship). And I always wear a fancy button-down Browns shirt the day after they win. (And yes, that shirt is still in almost-new condition).

Luckily, I'm not the only one behaving in such a way on my campus. One of my close friends is from Green Bay and is almost as much a fanatic as I am. The staff is also split between die-hard USC or UCLA fans (the primary Los Angeles rivalry)—and you can tell who is who from their classroom and dress during football season.

So why is this important? All of this home-team spirit is great for the students to see and enjoy. Besides making us "human," sports often gives us a subject—one outside of academia—that we can share with the students. Those students who habitually have problems in class, especially adolescent boys *and* girls, can often be "reached" through a discussion of sports. And once a relationship is established, it is so much easier to work with them on their academics. Through mutual sports interest, a trust and camaraderie can be established between you.

(Now granted, I always have a couple students who purposely wear a Pittsburg Steelers or a Michigan Wolverines shirt to my class—usually put up to it by a parent. That always provides me with a wonderful opportunity to threaten to abuse my teacher "power" for their "blasphemy.")

To promote college awareness at my school, every Wednesday is designated "college-shirt day." We have a uniform policy exemption for wearing a college shirt on that day. Many students start to personally affiliate with colleges that are promoted by the home-team spirit of their favorite teachers.

Supporting your home team in front of the students also teaches them it's okay to promote pride in organizations with which they identify. It naturally promotes school, classroom, or school club/team pride. But it also allows you to get them to express pride in their work in other areas. At my school, the last two principals would treat the spring standardized testing like a school football homecoming celebration. They organized "pep rallies" and songs and cheers, all involving the test-taking experience. One year, the principal had t-shirts made for every student with the Ghostbusters logo and the words "I ain't afraid of no test" on the front. The entire campaign was meant to get the students to take pride in their test-taking, do their best, and raise their attendance on the days of the test.

The students fully bought into the program, and our scores went up as a result of nothing more than injecting pride and team-support into their efforts. And this all started with teachers demonstrating how to take pride in their home teams.

This type of "team spirit" can also be extended to the classroom in the form of fun competitions or cooperative learning teams when appropriate. Use it to build pride for the school, for your classroom, and for the students' personal work.

The atmosphere you create in your classroom has more effect on your students' academic, social, and emotional achievement than you may ever realize or witness. Have fun and run with it. But not to the benefit of the Steelers or Wolverines, please.

11

Take Curricular Chances

"Once upon a time, teachers had the professional freedom to take curricular chances...."

I often begin my discussions with new teachers about the "good old days of education" with that clichéd line. However, one of the great things about the Common Core, as written, is that it restores curricular freedom for teachers. This corrects one of the most serious consequences of No Child Left Behind—the stifling of teacher creativity and the demand to teach with pre-made curricula or to strictly follow a pre-determined pacing plan. Thankfully, this has changed with the Common Core.

It's unfortunate—and at times difficult to comprehend—but teachers who began their teaching careers after 2002 have not taught in a climate where teacher-creativity and taking chances have been encouraged. That's a huge proportion of our current teaching staffs who have never been encouraged to incorporate their ingenuity, inventiveness, and adaptability to their classroom curricula.

Hopefully, we can get that to change.

An example: Years ago, supermarkets gave free turkeys to customers who spent a certain amount of money the week before Thanksgiving. Having a Kosher kitchen, we couldn't use the bird at home. But being a teacher, I couldn't pass up a free turkey.

During Thanksgiving week we had school for only three days—often three virtually useless days due to heavy absenteeism. So I had a brainstorm for putting the turkey to good use—a cooperative learning lesson.

On Monday morning, I put the turkey on the front table and went about taking attendance. The students naturally asked, "What's that?"

Me: "It's a turkey."

Students: "What's it for?"

Me: "That's up to you."

We then began a discussion as to what the turkey could be used for. Now understand, I had some ideas where this activity would go, but nothing solidly planned in advance. This was a spontaneous teaching opportunity. I was going to let my sixth-grade students determine the path that this unit would take. Hopefully, the experience would be enough to last three days!

Ultimately, after a lengthy discussion, my students decided to hold a Thanksgiving feast rather than donate the turkey to charity (the close second choice).

A subsequent discussion then ensued as to the work groups that they would need to organize for their project. The class decided on the following groups:

- **Cooking group**—Research how to cook the turkey.
- **Side dishes group**—Determine and research side dishes for the feast.
- **Research group**—Research the holiday, thereby ensuring a "curricular" context. They would report out as part of the "program."

- **Decoration group**—Create appropriate decorations for the classroom and invitations to guests.
- **Charity group**—Investigate local food banks and write up some information about them. All guests were going to be asked to bring a can of food to donate as admission. This was in lieu of donating the bird to charity.

The groups all worked beautifully for the next two days, and the feast was wonderful. In addition, there were some unexpected positive learning opportunities that came out of the experience:

- **A science lesson**—As we were cleaning the turkey, we ended up having a biology lesson investigating the bird's heart, liver, and neck.
- **A math lesson**—As we were discussing cooking side dishes (all of which were required to be homemade), we discussed adapting recipes for larger numbers. This led directly to a math lesson on multiplying fractions.
- **A cooking/physics lesson**—As I met with the cooking group at 6 a.m. in the cafeteria kitchen, I commented that it was a pity that gravity caused all of the juices to sink to the bottom of the bird, thereby drying out the breast on top and making the inedible back very moist. One of my students thought about my words, then suggested, "Why don't we turn the turkey upside down so the juices go into the turkey breast?" This obviously was exactly what I wanted to have done. And the white meat was juicy and delicious!

This unexpected, unplanned, improvised unit turned out to be a fantastic educational experience for my students! And all because I decided to take a chance with an unplanned "curricular deviation."

Another story of a successful, spontaneous lesson developed in my car on my way to school:

I was planning on teaching the concept of "setting" to my English class that day, using the same lesson I had used for years. While listening to the Sirius/XM Broadway station, I got a brainstorm. I realized that Broadway composers use their overtures to "set the stage" for their work. This was similar to an author using the first page of a book to "set the stage" for the story.

When I arrived at school, I searched for a number of Broadway CDs that had an overture that musically established the "setting" of the story. I selected: *Phantom of the Opera*, *Hairspray*, *Wicked*, *Spamalot*, *Avenue Q*, and *A Chorus Line*. I played the first minute or so of the shows and then asked my students what the show was about, based on the music/instrumentation the composers chose to promote the required mood for the piece. They were generally correct for each example. We then talked about how authors use specific words and phrases to convey a setting or mood for their stories. Ultimately, they wrote their own "opening paragraph" for a number of different genres: mystery, adventure, humor, romance, horror. Using the Broadway musical examples, they quickly comprehended the concept of literary setting.

In today's classrooms, teachers are expected to follow specific curricula tied to state standards. Earlier I mentioned the principal who cautioned our staff that "if it's not tested, I don't want it taught." However, we as professionals know what is best for our students; we know the material that the students need to know to be successful. And sometimes it may be educational experiences *not* tested. I can guarantee you, if asked by an administrator, I could locate a state standard for every aspect of my "turkey lesson" above—even if it were a spontaneous lesson. The Common Core standards are that broad and general. I guarantee that you can do the same for virtually any curricular innovation you incorporate into your classroom.

As a creative teacher, you will get "brainstorms." Follow up on them. Implement them. Take curricular chances. Some of the best lessons you will ever teach will be the result of your unique, spontaneous ideas.

And this is what often brings the "fun" back into teaching.

12

Administrators Want You To Succeed

Throughout my career, I've usually enjoyed excellent relationships with my school administrators. I've always viewed them as allies in the overall educational process. In turn, they've consistently provided me with the respect and academic freedom I've needed to do what I wanted to do with my students. This wonderful arrangement came as a result of developing a mutual trust between us, one in which my professional judgment was respected. My administrators knew that I always had the welfare of my students, and the school in general, in my heart and head, and they believed I was good at my job and could accomplish my educational goals. These relationships have helped make for a positive and usually fun environment at my various schools over the years. No teacher could ask for more.

As I said to my first principal, "I'm here for one year, but I'll stay as long as I'm enjoying myself." Here I am—thirty-some years later, still enjoying myself.

Now, what I just wrote may cause extreme rolling-of-the-eyes among more experienced teachers. Unfortunately, some teachers do not have great relationships with their administrators—even when they have a "good" principal and assistant principals. But throughout my career I have maintained that, contrary to the opinion of many teachers, administrators are not the enemy. In fact, in my work as a teacher union officer, I would classify as "good" the vast majority of the principals in my district. They are respectful of and collaborative with their staffs, proficient at their jobs, and they create a positive working environment at the school.

And if you're a new teacher, here's a news flash: Administrators want you to succeed.

Okay—sometimes it doesn't seem like it. I'll never forget my second day at my new school. One of the assistant principals came in to conduct a formal observation of my teaching. On my second day! Luckily, he was a friend of mine from before I even arrived at the school, and he said he did it in order to get a good evaluation on the record immediately. He sincerely thought he was doing me a favor. Consequently, I've kidded him for years about "terrorizing me" on the second day of class.

This is not meant to make light of the negative principals who have problematic relationships with teachers. But those type of relationships usually take time to develop—or, should I say, deteriorate. However, as I stated previously, the principal *really* wants you, as a new teacher in the school, to succeed.

Think about it. It actually makes a lot of sense. The principal hired you. Your success will make the principal look good; your failure will make the principal look bad. Therefore, it's in everyone's best interest to do whatever is necessary to help you succeed.

My father told me a story about when he was working for another lawyer early in his legal career. He was required to become an "expert" in a specialty related to a trial. Prior to court, he was making a presentation to his boss. One minute into the presentation, his boss stopped him and said, "I don't care about any of this stuff. You have one job to do, and one job only. Your job is to make me look good." My father realized that this was the basis of the employer-employee relationship.

And it's also the basis of a good teacher-principal relationship. Your job is to make the principal look good. Now, some explanation is needed about what "looking good" entails. High test scores make a principal "look good," but that's not what I'm talking about. I'm referring to when your teaching becomes a source of pride for your principal; when you are considered a significant asset to the school. I'm referring to your contribution to having the school be considered a positive, valuable part of the community. That's the ultimate "looking good' for a principal in the role of the educational leader of the institution.

When you make a principal "look good," that principal will extend to you more academic freedom and trust to allow you to do your best and thus accomplish that goal. It's truly a symbiotic relationship. As a result, in every interview I've ever had with a new principal, I've always said, "My job is to make you look good." The principal has continually appreciated that position, and has subsequently provided me with the freedom to do what I have felt is right. (This isn't to say that all of my administrators have been wonderful. But in all these years I've come across just one exception to this rule: one principal—perhaps the least effective principal I've ever had—who answered me, "I don't need anyone to make me look good.")

A good, trusting relationship with your administrator alleviates a great deal of stress. Teachers too often panic when an administrator walks into the room. I believe that this reaction is very misguided. I've always loved when administrators come into my room to observe, as it provides me with a great opportunity to show off my stuff! And if you have a good relationship with the person, you can often get some good tips on how to improve your lesson. Remember—the administrator was once a teacher like you, and should have both knowledge and experience to share!

For example, there are certain special lessons that I teach throughout the year that represent some of my best work. I will often invite an administrator to my class to watch the lesson, not to critique it, but simply to observe it. These people enjoy good teaching! They enjoy innovative lessons. Unfortunately, it's rare for administrators to get into classrooms to watch their teachers unless it's a required formal observation or to address a problem. They're too busy with paperwork and administrative duties to really take the time to enjoy their teaching staff. That's one reason they love to come in and watch some of my special lessons.

And they mark on their calendar in advance the day I have my annual International Food Faire, and they skip breakfast.

These invited visitations are not evaluative, and are meant to be fun. However, there was one incident I had that kind of backfired on me. I invited one of the assistant principals in to watch the special English lesson on "setting" that I mentioned above. This is the lesson where I use Broadway overtures to demonstrate to my students how orchestrations create the setting for a musical, similar to an author's word choice on the first page to create the setting for a story. I invited this administrator because I knew how much she enjoyed Broadway shows. The next day, she unexpectedly called me into her office and handed me three handwritten, legal-size, yellow sheets of notes from what she observed! I chided her that this wasn't an "observation" and that she was simply there to enjoy herself. She reminded me that she was a habitual note-taker. (I always teased her about that event, and when I was Master of Ceremonies for her retirement party, I presented her with pages of yellow legal pad notes on her administrative work. Just for fun.)

A good, trusting relationship with your administrator also serves you well on your formal evaluation, which you are sure to experience in your first few years of teaching. These evaluations are highly subjective. As a result, no matter how wonderful a lesson may be, any administrator will find a great deal to criticize, focus on, or suggest what "you could have done but failed to do...." However, it's important to remember that the reverse is also true. A good, trusting relationship with an administrator can also lead to the evaluator actively searching for the positive in an observation. Remember, administrators want you to be a success, and you need to work with that in mind.

On the flip side of the administrator/teacher relationship, and almost as a contradiction to what I stated above, you need to always remember that the administrator is not your "friend." You can be on friendly terms with your administrators: you can socialize with them, go to Happy Hours, dinner, etc. But always remember that professionally, you have separate, distinct roles. The administrator is your supervisor and is, in turn, responsible to district supervisors.

Along these lines, it's wise to not be friends with administrators on Facebook and other social media. Remember that when you share posts with your administrators, their friends can see them, too—and their friends often include higher-level district personnel. You don't want to put yourself in a potentially negative position by allowing them to view personal posts you wouldn't want your boss to see.

Another bit of advice. Whenever possible, approach your fellow teachers with questions or problems before you go to an administrator. It isn't that the administrators do not want to help you. It's that the district often makes them spend ridiculous amounts of time getting all of their administrative tasks completed—one reason I'm still in the classroom, and not an administrator. The more you need their attention, the more they cannot tend to their own responsibilities. On some critical issues, yes, approach them—that's why they are there. But if you're "bothering them" continuously, that's going to end up being problematic for you.

So what's my overall message in this chapter? Try to enjoy a good relationship with your administrators. They sincerely want you to succeed and will do whatever they can to encourage that to happen. Share your good teaching with them, your innovation, your creativity. Go ahead and show off a bit. Listen to their advice when you feel it's appropriate and helpful.

It's really a simple, basic concept: the more positive your relationship with your boss, the more you'll enjoy your job. And the various administrators I've worked with throughout my career are a significant reason that I'm still enjoying this work after so many years.

13

Beware of Smoke Machines

In a previous chapter I talked about taking curricular chances. And when you take chances, sometimes new ideas work well, and sometimes they flame out. But that's not a bad thing, because I also believe that a teacher who never fails, never tries anything new.

However, I need to add a note of caution. Be careful when you try something absolutely new or totally out of the ordinary. Unexpected consequences may result. Sometimes they work out great—sometimes not so much.

I know that I'm presenting a bit of a dichotomy—that is, be creative, but always prepare for the unexpected, and learn how to roll with it.

My best stories of unexpected consequences revolve around two smoke machines.

While teaching elementary school many years ago, I put on a musical theater production where a "cat" was going to "heaven" at the very end of the show. It was very dramatic—she walks up a ramp lined with colored lights tilted to add perspective, and it's somewhat dark. The effect was quite impressive.

After the first night of the show, my outside videographer offered to let us use his smoke machine in order to improve the effect. A stage crew student would sit behind the back end of the ramp and, at the appropriate time, would turn on the machine and produce a “fog” that would slowly spread out from under the ramp like a “cloud.” We tested it and determined that the operator would hold the button and count to five and then release, thus producing the perfect amount of smoke.

And soon after, we learned about the unexpected consequences of live theater.

Late in the show that night, when the smoke was to be turned on, the operator did exactly what she was supposed to do—hold the button down for five seconds and release. However, the “cat” at the top of the ramp didn’t see any smoke coming out, since we planned for it to collect under the ramp and slowly move out. So she whispered to the operator, “More smoke! More smoke!” Well, the student working the machine listened to her, and pushed the button for another five seconds.

This happened three more times in succession.

Needless to say, within 30 seconds, an eight-foot wall of smoke started to move slowly toward the audience, engulfing all of the cast members as they sang.

Knowing the importance of the teacher reacting quickly in a crisis, I immediately left my director post and ran through the smoke to open all of the auditorium doors and calm a couple students who were beginning to shout.

The cloud quickly dissipated, the song ended without further incident, and the audience had a good laugh at the end when I explained what happened.

And I swore never to put something that new into the middle of a show—or the middle of a lesson—without fully trying it out under optimum conditions.

But sometimes trying something new works out unexpectedly well, though it often can’t be duplicated because of the unique conditions surrounding the first time.

Many years after the "smoke" incident, my Pacoima Singers were performing the number "Defying Gravity" from *Wicked*. We had our Elphaba, and a manually operated lift (think of a big metal teeter-totter hidden by a curtain). At the appropriate time, replicating what occurred in the Broadway production, she was lifted about four feet into the air, as if she were flying. To add to the effect, we had a smoke machine running behind her that enveloped her in smoke that had been turned green by our lighting. It really "wowed" the audience.

However, on closing night, the smoke was unexpectedly different. Instead of enveloping her, it rose and formed a flat layer across the stage at her feet, as if she were standing on a green cloud. Watching it later on video, it was a remarkable effect. When I asked Stage Crew afterward how they did it—how they were able to stop the smoke exactly at her feet—the answer was unexpected. It turns out that the student in charge of the smoke machine forgot to turn it on to heat it up, and was actually very late in doing so. The smoke *accidently* rose only to that exact height, since the machine was not sufficiently warmed up. Thus the crew couldn't reproduce the effect even if they wanted to.

So—what's the theme of this chapter? Be creative, but beware of trying off-the-wall things with your students. Try using new teaching ideas, but prepare for unexpected consequences—positive and negative.

Don't forget: that's part of the fun of working with kids!

14

Why I Refuse to Use an Online Grading Program

If something works for you and your students—even if it's not "popular"—use it or do it. It may be "old fashioned" or "off the wall"—it doesn't matter. If you, in your professional opinion, think that it works for you, incorporate it into your teaching or classroom. That's the basis of my justification for why I refuse to use an online grading program.

However, a disclaimer is needed before you continue with this chapter. Many teachers *love* online grading programs. They think they're easy and helpful, and so swear by them. If you're one of those people, you may want to skip this chapter.

As you've probably surmised, I'm not one of those people.

Almost every bit of writing I do at school or at home is on a computer. It's been that way for decades—ever since the Apple IIc and my 5 ¼" floppy disks. That said, the only thing that I do NOT do on the computer is my grades.

I know, many of you are thinking that that is crazy, especially with all of the grading programs available nowadays. In fact, a couple of years ago, when my district stopped ordering those blue, half-page grade sheets, I hoarded a couple hundred of them before they could be destroyed, as I had every intention of keeping my archaic black, three-ring roll book as long as humanly possible.

In fact, at a recent union board meeting, I was finishing my grades, and a number of my peers stopped by to laugh at me for still doing them by hand.

So why am I still a grading dinosaur?

I have more control with my grades in handwritten form. For example, I will generally throw out the lowest grade if I have ten or more of the same type of assignment. I have a "reputation" of being really hard on my students (three times over the past twenty years my sixth-grade students got together and produced "I Survived Dr. Mandel's Class" t-shirts). With my handwritten roll book, if they mess up once or twice over the course of a grading period, I can compensate—without having to reprogram the grading equations!

For the sixth grade, I use grades as a positive motivator and to show the parents where their child truly stands academically. If a student is an A/B student, I don't feel that one or two poor grades should change that assessment. Sixth grade is the beginning of middle school; the students have multiple teachers, the material is harder, and assignments are at times difficult for them.

As I mentioned in an earlier chapter, as a result of a conference with the parent of a student with academic problems, I will make them a deal: If they turn in the rest of his or her work, at a "C" or higher level, I will throw out the previous bad grades.

I can't have that freedom with a programmed grade computer system without spending significant time reprogramming or going into the program and making click- and delete-type adaptations.

For example, last year I had a student who was living with her mom and brother in a battered-women's shelter. Not only was it difficult for her to study and do her work at night with the crowd there, but this eleven-year-old took three subways and buses to get to school. She was receiving an "F" in her other classes—even though her records showed that she had been a good student in the fifth grade. I made a deal with her: If she got 80% of her assignments turned in, and they were complete, she would get at least a "C" from me.

I can't easily do that with a computer grade program (although I'm told that some of the newer programs have override capabilities that allow a teacher to put in a different grade than what the system determines; still, for me personally, it's not as easy as using the roll book).

My roll book also makes it easier to answer a student's question about grades. I asked a friend who swears by his online grading program to go through the process of showing me a student's grades. Little did he know I was timing him. From the time I asked him to see the grades, he had to boot up the program, do a search, and show me the grades—it took about two minutes. I then timed myself from the time a parent "asked" me about a grade. The time it took me to reach over, get my roll book, open up to the child's class and show the parent the grades:

12 seconds.

One last, very hot topic about computer grade programs: There is a big push now to have grade programs post grades online, thereby making them accessible to a parent at any time.

I am 100% against that procedure. I do NOT want a parent having that access without speaking to me! I want to retain the ability to explain the child's progress; to explain why the grades are the way they are. I want to explain the factors that are involved—such as classroom behavior and work habits—and whether the child can make up a grade or not. A "B" for one student may be a great grade, but for another it's a disappointment. This is the whole reason we have parent conferences. A parent who has easy access to all grades without putting them into perspective invites problems for the teacher, and worse, may feel that there is no need for a traditional face-to-face conference with the teacher.

But what about the parent who doesn't want to wait until a conference or grade report to come home? There's a ready solution to this.

Write me a note; send me an email with the question: "How is my child doing?" An answer will come either by note or phone call—with any necessary explanation—within 24 hours.

So let them laugh at me as I do my grades by hand. (I'm actually pretty fast with a calculator.) It works for me. And that is my primary advice to all teachers:

If it works for you and your students, do it.

15

Numbers Don't Always Add Up—And Fair Grades Take Some Effort

Grading is one of the most powerful tools that teachers have—and it's also an abused and misused one. A teacher's grade determination is usually final. Teachers are often protected by state laws that prohibit any administrator from changing their grades. On the other hand, grades are too often the only aspect of the child's education that a parent truly cares about. Thus, the teacher is in a very advantageous position. But it's important to remember the Peter Parker Principle: "With great power comes great responsibility."[1] It was good advice for Spiderman, and it's good advice for teachers.

This chapter won't delve into how to figure out your grades. There are other books dedicated to teaching that skill.[2] Rather, the chapter is going to reflect on the basic concepts of grading and the ramifications of a teacher's actions concerning grading. And those ramifications can be substantial and often unknown to the teacher.

Unfortunately, there are several ways in which teachers

1 Lee (1962). Amazing Fantasy #15. New York: Marvel Comics.

2 See Mandel (2009) for a detailed discussion on how to figure out your grades.

abuse or misuse grades. First, when teachers abuse the grading process, their rationale is that they are manipulating grades for a "nobler" purpose. My school has four ten-week report cards and a five-week progress report in between. The purpose of the progress report is to inform the parents that their child is in danger of receiving a "D", "F", or "U" on a ten-week report ("U" for "Unsatisfactory" in "work habits" or "cooperation"). I've worked with teachers who—on principle—will give 90% of their classes "D's" and "F's" on the first progress report for no other reason than to motivate their students! However, they never see the punishment that many of these students have to endure as a result of bringing home a grade of this type. Worse for me personally is when parents decide to pull their child out of my singing group because they have determined that their child needs to spend all of his or her time on tutoring or just working because of the "D" or "F" they received from those teachers! It's a blatant abuse of the grading system. And, unfortunately, no one can do anything about it, as classroom teachers have the final say on their grades. (It's gotten so bad that I actually have to warn parents at my opening meeting to expect that grade on the first progress report, so as to not react negatively.)

Second, there are teachers who do not truly understand the basic grading process. Too often this happens with relatively new teachers who incorporate a point system. In many cases the students receive final grades well below what they should have earned. And when the teacher is questioned about the grade, the teacher simply adds up the points the student received, compares the result to the scale, and justifies the grade that was recorded.

However, there's a fatal flaw in this logic. For example, one of my students was very frustrated because she was receiving a "D-" in her class based on two tests—she earned an "A" on one, and an "F" on the other. The two tests were supposed to be equally weighted. I asked the teacher about it, and she showed me that the girl received a 96 on one test and only a 24 on the other. Averaged out, she showed me that they came to a 60, which was a "D-" in her class.

Although I pointed out that logic dictates that an "A" and an "F" should average out to a "C", the teacher was adamant that her math was correct. And therein lies the problem with using a straight point system to grade: "F" grades are unfairly weighted. "A's" to "D's" generally have a ten-point spread (90-100 , 80-89, 70-79, 60-69), yet an F has a significantly larger one (0-59).

I gently shared this flaw with the teacher and suggested that she program any "F" grade lower than 50 as a "50" in her computer. (This is another reason why I don't like online grade books, as I discussed in the previous chapter). The physical test itself can have the numerical mark that was earned—the 24 in this case—but when the final grades are *calculated,* all low "F's" are given the same weight as other grades.

Following this adaptation, the student mentioned above would have her grades calculated as 96 and 50, which averages out to a 73—a "C"—which is the grade she *should* have if receiving an "A" and an "F". It's really that simple.

And that leads to my primary message about grading: Be Fair. Children should get the grade that reflects their work, their knowledge of the material, and the progress they have displayed in class. My son had what I, to this day, consider an unfair Algebra II teacher. One-hundred percent of her students' grades were based on the tests she gave. My son did all of his homework, understood all of the material, participated in class—and had horrible test anxiety. As a result, he received an "F" in her class and had to re-take the course in summer school. We even got him a tutor—who was frustrated because he continually insisted that my son understood the material and we were wasting his time. Because this teacher only took into account her tests in grading, he still flunked the class. And there was nothing anyone could do about it. That's blatantly unfair grading.

As a teacher, I regularly throw out a single bad test grade if it's an outlier from the student's normal achievement. Everyone has a bad day. Everyone occasionally has a bad test. If an outlier grade doesn't reflect the student's overall progress, get rid of it in your final calculations! Do what's right—be fair.

I also make special allowances for students in rare circumstances. For example, I had a fantastic student in my English class. Her work was well above average in every aspect of my class, from reading comprehension to writing skills. In fact, she was earning "A's" in all of her classes. However, she couldn't spell no matter what. It had been an ingrown weakness throughout her schooling. The best she could do, with studying, was a high "D" on my weekly spelling tests. Unfortunately for her, spelling accounted for 25% of the English grade in my class. If I "followed the rules," this straight-"A" student would receive a "B". Therefore, I told her and her mother during our parent conferences that as long as she tried and received at least a "D" on my tests—I would throw out the final spelling grade and she would get the grade she really deserved. Do what's right—be fair.

There's a practice I always use when I'm done figuring out my grades. I look over all of the grades that the student has earned throughout the period, and I do a quick estimation in my head. This tells me the grade the student probably "should" have. I then compare it with the grade I calculated. If they match, great. If they don't, I recalculate the grade to ascertain where I was off. I may have been off with the estimation—but I may have also been off with the calculation.

Finally—and this has assisted me more times than I care to imagine—I look at all "C's", "D's", "F's", and "U's" and pretend that the parent has come in for a conference and is questioning my grade. Can I justify it? If I have the data in my grade book to justify the grade, fantastic. But if I discover a flaw in my logic, I go back and rethink and recalculate the grade I gave that student.

Being fair is paramount to both good and bad grades. I'll never forget my first year in my school district. I gave a fourth-grader four "D's" and an "F"—and his parents thanked me! Evidently, I was the first teacher to give their son the grades he actually deserved.

I cannot stress enough the concept of being fair and giving the grades that the child truly earns. I always say to my students that they are not to thank me for giving them an "A"—I wasn't responsible for that grade, the student was. Simultaneously, I'm not to blame for a student's "D" or "F"—the student is also responsible for that grade. All I do is determine the grade that best describes the student's progress and that is fair. Nothing more, nothing less. "With great power comes great responsibility."

16

Don't Fill Your Car Trunk with Your In-Service Class

A number of years ago, I purchased a new car and gave my old one to my college-age son. As I was cleaning out the car before handing it over, I felt tinges of nostalgia. In the trunk was a collection of handouts and materials from in-service classes/sessions I had attended over the previous eight years. As I sorted through the material, I remembered all of the sessions and all of the ideas I was going to try one day when I had time. It was like revisiting a personal professional development scrapbook.

I sighed as I collected the old material and gently deposited it in the trash can.

Workshops—and especially salary point classes—can be quite helpful, and they can also be horrible wastes of time. Unfortunately, our educational pay system is one where, in order to advance up the salary scale, you must take classes to "improve." Please know that this is different from virtually every other profession, wherein required "in-service" is self-determined and self-reported.

The worst classes are the ones where the instructor has a significant ego—where the "homework" is nothing more than busywork, fulfilling whatever requirements that he or she deems personally important, regardless of whether or not it has any relevance to your professional life.

Each year, I teach three two-day salary point classes, along with numerous workshops. The workshops all have multiple handouts for the teachers, and the salary point classes all require homework for the participants—exactly the type of materials I threw out from my old car.

The thought of my salary point class material becoming landfill is troublesome. Therefore, when I give out homework in my salary point classes, I have one important rule. The project MUST be something that the participant is going to use that year, or in the coming school year. In other words, the result of my assignments must be relevant to the teachers' professional lives. That is my one hard-and-fast rule. I don't care what the project subject is (I always teach methodology classes rather than subject-matter-specific topics), and I don't care what format they use for their homework. In fact, I tell them to use whatever format they normally use in their curricular planning. All I care about is that the material they create will be incorporated into a classroom and that their time with me will not be wasted. (Granted—their frustration is sometimes amusing as they try to pin me down on specific formats.)

When I present my workshops and discussions, I make sure that the examples I use are taken directly from the participants' curricular lives. When I begin a session, the first thing I do is go around the room asking the participants' grade levels and subject areas. I then adapt all of my examples to match their various teaching situations.

The key to this philosophy is professional respect. When you lead your fellow teachers, it's critical that you show them respect for their teaching knowledge and experiences. The most important way of doing this is to demonstrate to them that you feel that their time is valuable. Unfortunately, I am quite aware that few, if any, of the participants are taking my courses because of my "brilliant presentations" or to share in my "abundant knowledge." They're there to acquire a salary point and move up the scale. Therefore, I want them to at least feel that their time with me was somewhat beneficial and not a waste.

We are all so busy as it is. If you ever find yourself a leader of teacher professional development, make sure that if you need the participants to produce some work for you, that the product is relevant and useful to them, so that their time has been well spent.

17

Special Ed Kids Are Like Everyone Else

My wife is a special education teacher. She has a special day class of learning-disabled elementary students, grades 4 and 5. In fact, we met when I was teaching elementary school, and I was the only one willing to have her students mainstreamed into my classroom.

I've always found it amazing how some teachers look down on special ed kids. They often avoid them like the plague and frequently blame school problems on these students. Personally, I have always found that attitude to be horribly misplaced.

Special Ed kids are like everyone else—they simply have a learning disability. Once that difficulty is compensated for, they should be able to work on a level comparable to their peers, and often blossom when treated as such.

I always say that I, too, have a learning disability. I am so nearsighted I cannot function successfully in a classroom without some compensation—in my case, glasses. However, glasses are a "socially accepted" compensation. Most intellectual difficulties are not.

My favorite story of special ed students being successful goes back to my elementary school days when I was incorporating cooperative learning into my curriculum. I had four special ed students in my classroom, and all of them were active, successful participants in cooperative learning experiences. One day, I had my principal observe the session—she was not a big fan of cooperative learning at the time—and I challenged her to identify the four special ed students. She sat at my desk for about ten minutes stymied, then walked around the room observing every group. After twenty minutes, she guessed one of them—but could not identify the other three. The special ed students were totally, successfully integrated into the classroom lesson.

As a teacher, you can have a profound effect on special ed students simply by believing in them and accepting, valuing, and appreciating them for who they are. I'm a strong advocate of the concept of the self-fulfilling prophecy. Students will raise themselves up—or lower themselves down—to the level that you expect from them. This is especially relevant with special education students, who are routinely "looked down upon" and treated as if they are "less valuable and capable" than others.

Here are a couple of examples of the benefits of that self-fulfilling prophecy.

At my middle school, in my gifted English/history sixth-grade class, I was assigned a student who had a severe emotional disturbance. He had a one-on-one aide with him at all times. I was warned about his behavior at his elementary school—he physically assaulted the principal and necessitated the police being called on him a number of times. His father was even banned from the school.

The strategy I used with this student was to sit him down the very first day and inform him that I knew about his history at his previous school, and that I didn't believe he was "that bad." I explained to him that I expected the same behavior from him as I did from the other students.

The compensation I made for his disability was that when he felt that he was going to explode, he had my permission to walk out of the classroom, just outside the door, to calm himself down. He was required to say to me that he needed "private time," and he was allowed to exit and get himself back to where he needed to be emotionally. In addition, I would not allow his one-on-one aide to interact with him in the classroom. He didn't need her for academia (he was the highest-level student in the gifted class), but rather for behavior problems. I wanted to wean him off of the aide and to eliminate the middle school social stigma of having an adult follow him around all day.

The result of this plan was that his tantrums became fewer and fewer, and within a few months the aide's time was gradually phased out.

By eighth grade this student was totally without his one-on-one, and his tantrums were non-existent. He was completely written out of special education, and he went off to high school, just like any other student.

Coda to the story—the next year I was assigned another student considered "emotionally disturbed" from the same elementary school. She, too, excelled as a result of being expected to comply with the same academic and behavioral expectations made of the other students. It led us to conclude that the problem was more the attitudes of this particular elementary school than it was the students!

Okay—one more story. (I can't help myself—I love special ed success stories, since normally all you hear about are special ed problems.) My first year in the district I taught fourth grade, and I was assigned to the school about three weeks into the year. I was given a class that included Student Y. Student Y suffered from very serious emotional disturbances. The way the school had handled her up until then was to send her to the office every day and allow her to hang out there as long as she wanted. If she threw a temper tantrum, she was immediately sent home.

The first week, Student Y left my class and went to the office without my permission. When I went to get her at recess, she started screaming and swearing at me inside the office. The secretaries jumped up to "save" this new teacher from her, but I put my hand up for them to stay out of it. I folded my arms and let Student Y yell and swear at me for about ten minutes.

When she was done, and crying from exhaustion, I asked her, "Are you done?"

She said, "Yes."

I replied, "Good. Let's go back to class." She followed me out without another word.

Not once for the remainder of the year did Student Y get sent to the office, nor did she ever leave without permission. We developed a system where she came up to me and said, "I need to go out, I'm losing control." She would go out of the room and return within minutes. By the end of the year, she was behaving as "normally" as any of the other kids.

All of these are examples of the self-fulfilling prophecy. If you believe that special education students can, and should, succeed, chances are better than not that—with the proper educational modifications, of course—they will.

Special education students are like anyone else. They simply have a deficiency or discrepancy in some area. Too often their "negative" behaviors are the result of the "self-fulfilling prophecy"—they are acting as they believe the adults in contact with them expect them to behave. Whereas the "self-fulfilling prophecy" is applicable to all of our students, I have found through the years that it's even more prevalent when dealing with special education students, who all too often already have a "stigma" attached to them. They need our understanding and acceptance, and our high expectations that they can function like anyone else once compensation has been made for their educational problem.

Once that is done, you will find that special ed kids are like everyone else, and that they're some of the most "special" students you'll ever have.

18

So Are Non-English Speakers

Most Professional Development sessions are useful and well taught. However, sometimes there are clunkers. Occasionally there's one that can actually rile you. I remember one such episode to this day.

We were attending a mandatory PD session on how to teach with the new history book (because heaven forbid, "we experienced teachers couldn't figure out how to use a new textbook," he said sarcastically).

The facilitator was introducing us to a supplemental activity for the Ancient Egypt unit. She was demonstrating that the students could write "postcards home from Egypt" to their parents. She explained how the students can write about their "experiences" in Ancient Egypt on one side of the card. She then went on to point out how our gifted students could fill up both sides of the card—and that our English Language Learners (ELL) students could write a couple of sentences on one side in their native language.

Needless to say, my reaction to this difference in expectations was significant. While it's true that many ELL students may have below-grade-level skills in their native language, the vast majority are proficient in their home tongue. Therefore, if ELLs were writing in their own language, the expectations should be the same as for English-speaking students! To expect anything less could be considered unprofessional!

A small minority of teachers believe that non-English speaking is synonymous with lower ability and is therefore met with lower expectations. A non-English speaker is simply that: someone who does not speak English. Nothing more, nothing less.

For those of us who remember Bi-Lingual Education, the philosophy that ELL students are as intelligent as English speakers formed the basis of the program. In Bi-Lingual Education, a teacher teaches non-English speakers in their native language, in their core subjects, during the two years it normally takes to learn English. That way, the ELL student doesn't fall behind academically while simultaneously learning English.

In the previous chapter, I discussed how Special Education students are intelligent and capable. They just have different processing issues—a learning discrepancy—that must be addressed. The cognitive level of ELLs is not related to their language deficiency. In many ways, a number of the concepts shared in the chapter on Special Education are applicable here as well.

For example, ELLs excel in Cooperative Group Work, just as Special Education students do when you account for their language difficulty.[1] This can be accomplished a number of ways:

- You can pair up a student with a "translator."
- You can use Google Translate (*translate.google.com*) to translate materials that the groups will use.
- You can also allow a group of similar speakers to carry on their discussions and to create their projects in their native language.

---

1 For an extensive discussion on working with ELLs within a Cooperative Group Work experience, see Mandel (2003).

In all three of these adaptations, the students' cognitive participation should be at the same level as the participating English speakers once you account for the language discrepancy.

My experience with ELL students began in my first year in my school district, when I was assigned a fourth-grade class. I had four ELLs on my roster. (Back then they were called ESL—English as a Second Language.) One spoke Spanish, one spoke Hebrew, one was fluent in Chinese, and one's native language was Korean. I subsequently approached my principal and asked her if she could assign English speakers to my classroom who were also fluent in each of those languages. Luckily, we had fourth-grade students who fit each of those language categories. I assigned them as "buddies," seating next to the corresponding ELL learner. The English speaker was able to translate for the ELL student in everything we did. Not only did the ELL student understand what was going on in class, but he was able to fully participate in all group discussions and activities. After a few days, the translating became a very normal component of the classroom. And within a couple of months, the ELL student was beginning to work on his own, in English. By the end of the year, the ELL student was certified as an English-speaker.

Whereas this "buddy system" worked in fourth grade, I wouldn't try it with either much younger students or with students older than sixth or seventh grade. Problems often develop when the students become teenagers, as social aspects may disrupt the "buddy" relationship if the two partners don't move in the same social circle. However, if the two are friends, and their partnership is entirely voluntary, the "buddy system" will most likely work in secondary classrooms.

One of my favorite ELL success stories happened quite by accident. Every teacher develops certain strengths and weaknesses over the years. There are certain ages and types of students you do really well with, and certain ones that are more of a challenge. This is especially true in elementary school, where you have the same students all day, or in sixth grade, where you have them for extended periods with block scheduling. Over the years, I've developed a reputation as a teacher to whom an administrator could assign students representing every major behavioral problem in the grade—as long as they spoke English. My specialty has always been behavioral-problem students. Unfortunately, on the other side, I was weakest with ELL students. I've never had the extraordinary patience needed to be a successful ELL teacher. As a result, I always had to work harder with ELLs in my class, as this wasn't my forte. My ELLs still had a solid education, as discussed above. But to have an entire ELL classroom would most likely take me several years in which to become truly proficient.

My story comes from the one year my district decided to try to even out the vacation time students experienced. I was teaching elementary school when they made Winter Vacation six weeks long, from Thanksgiving through New Year's, and took the time off of Summer Vacation, making it six weeks long as well. To assist the students with continuity, they created a three-week Intersession Program, mostly for ELL and Special Education students. Being a fairly young teacher at the time and the father of small children, I needed the extra money, so I applied to teach Intersession. I was given an ELL class. Now, this was thirty years ago, before No Child Left Behind and the proliferation of scripted, mandated curricula. In fact, for the Intersession, I was given no curricula to follow. I was just told to develop my own in order to keep these students working on their English over vacation. This was actually the norm back them.

Anyway, not being an experienced ELL teacher (having only a few ELL students every year, not an entire class), I took a very novel approach. I showed my students "kid" videos in English every day. These movies contained stories and characters that they recognized. After each movie, the students had to draw a picture depicting one of the characters or scenes from the story. When this was completed, they were required to explain their picture to the rest of the class—in English. In addition, they were forced to speak English anytime they were in class, and out on the yard at recess. My program seemed to work. I didn't know how much they "formally" progressed, because there were no pre- or post-tests. However, the students all fully participated throughout the three-week session and seemed to enjoy learning English.

About a month afterward, I met a couple of their teachers at a meeting. They were gushing—they couldn't believe that these ELL students I had had for a three-week Intersession had become English speakers in such a short time. They kept pushing me to share my secret—and when I did, they didn't believe me!

Granted, in today's educational environment, one centered on testing and scripted intervention programs, there's no way I could ever get away with something that unorthodox. But back then I could be creative, and it worked. The students readily learned English when the subject matter involved something in which they were interested and that they enjoyed. Maybe that concept can still be applied to ELL students today....

Too often, ELL students are kept from participating in extracurricular activities. This is a huge mistake. Not only do they have a lot to offer, but extracurricular activities both encourage English learning and help socialize them to the school culture. In one of my first years at my elementary school, I ran a Musical Theater program after school. We performed an original show entitled *Age of Aquarius*, and I gave the opening solo—the song *Aquarius*—to an ELL student who literally knew no English at all. However, he sang the song perfectly in English and fully participated in the entire show. By the end of the school year, he was fluent in English and was one of the most popular students in his grade level.

I guess the reason my ELL students do well is the same reason my Special Education students succeed—I believe in the Self-Fulfilling Prophecy. I believe that students raise—or lower—themselves to the teacher's expectations. Students want to please their teachers. Therefore, they will do what the Teacher expects, good or bad. If you truly believe that the student will succeed, chances are the child will meet that expectation. But the opposite is also true. Low expectations will often lead to poor results. I find this self-fulfilling prophecy to be especially true with both ELL and Special Education students, who often have teachers with pre-conceived notions of their abilities, whether they be high or low.

Think about my opening anecdote. If you believe that ELL and Special Education students can and will do well once you adapt to their personal situation—they will. And that's a critical philosophy for any teacher to remember and act upon.

19

Leadership as a Student Trait

As I stated in my introduction, this book is largely built on the stories I would tell during my teacher in-service classes. Some of those stories were derived from my perspective on various teaching methodologies and philosophies I've learned over the years. These are mostly items that are not usually found in most teacher education books, but come from years of real experience in actual classrooms. Unfortunately, most teacher education books, along with district-provided in-service sessions, come from educators who haven't been in an actual classrooms in years—and often decades. There is a significant discrepancy between what they *think* will work and what actually *will* work.

Why am I including in this book these next two chapters centered on teaching methodology? Because they relate directly to my philosophy of teaching and educational research: that is, if the material isn't directly applicable to the classroom, the material is worthless. These two chapters are meant to share some educational curricular ideas that you may not have learned in your teacher education classes or district professional development sessions. Rather, this is day-to-day teaching reality that I've observed and learned over the years and feel the need to share.

Some quick background on the topic of this chapter: My dissertation research at USC was based on Cooperative Learning. Cooperative Learning had already been established as a highly successful and worthwhile teaching methodology. However, up to this point, most Cooperative Learning work required the teacher to change her teaching style to fit a Cooperative Learning model. In practice, few teachers were willing to do that.

As an alternative, my research goal was to discover *why* Cooperative Learning actually works—what are the basic concepts that the average teacher can take and apply to her personal classroom and established teaching style. I used a participant-observation method. In other words, I studied my own classroom.

One of the most significant findings that came out of my dissertation research was how the "Leadership Variable" is a primary component of our students' personality and subsequent classroom—and school—behavior. In brief, it was discovered that every student can be placed in one of three categories[1]:

LEADER—Initiates all discussion and work in groups.

FOLLOWER—Readily participates, but only after a leader initiates.

NON-PARTICIPANT—Will not voluntarily participate; is on task, but will not offer anything to the group unless asked or prodded.

---

1 See Mandel, S. (2003). *Cooperative work groups: Preparing students for the real world.* Thousand Oaks, CA: Corwin Press.

Although my research was limited to group work within the classroom lessons, these findings were easily transferable to other parts of classroom and school behavior.

Displays of these three types of student leadership behavior are prevalent throughout the school day. For example, do you ever have a student who raises his hand for *every* question you ask? Now, he knows he doesn't have the correct answer; you know he doesn't have the correct answer. But he raises that hand anyway. Why does he do this? Because he has a strong leadership personality trait that *requires* him to participate, no matter what.

At the opposite end of the spectrum, do you ever call on someone you think is off-task, who never raises his hand, and you try to catch him unprepared? And then, to your dismay, he always fools you and has the correct answer? That student has a non-participant personality style. He doesn't like to participate, but he is still on-task. "Non-participation" does not mean "off task"!

The implications of this phenomenon are significant. For example, if you grade for "classroom participation," you are actually grading the students' leadership personality. You are rewarding someone who—based solely on his personality—has to raise his hand and be heard, whether or not he's prepared or even on task. And, conversely, you are punishing a student who—again because of his personality—doesn't readily volunteer, although he may be completely engaged in the lesson.

Students with a high leadership personality have to lead, one way or another. Unlike adults who can control the "urge," students cannot. And if the student cannot lead in a "positive" manner, then it will be in a "negative" manner.

I maintain that the vast majority of gang leaders in our schools are students with strong leadership personalities who could not find a way to channel that leadership into a positive avenue. I further maintain that possibly the best way to stop the proliferation of high school gangs is to reestablish formal sports programs in middle and junior high schools so that these kids can find a positive way to lead and participate at an early age.

An example of this "negative" leadership personality stands out from my days teaching sixth grade in elementary school. We had twin boys who were "terrors." Literally every day in fifth grade, they would be in the office. In sixth grade, one was in a special education full day class, and the other in a resource program, mainstreamed into my class.

The special ed teacher and I sat them down at the beginning of the school year and discussed with them how we knew their reputation and didn't care. We liked them, recognized that they were leaders, and wanted to give them a fresh start. However, they had to make a decision whether or not they were going to be "positive" or "negative" leaders this year. They informed us that they would think about it and get back to us.

The next day, the two boys asked to meet with us. They had discussed it and decided that they wanted to be "positive" leaders. That decision affected virtually all their behavior the following year. They continually made positive choices and were willing to accept positive roles that we offered them. As a result, neither one of them was ever sent to the office. In fact, in my after-school musical theater program, both of them were such great role models that they became group officers for the year!

It is important that you recognize the Leadership Variable within your students and its effect on your classroom participation. Those classified as "followers" will do fine and participate as needed. For those classified as "non-participants," you can adapt your expectations knowing that they are on-task, but too uncomfortable to actively participate.

But most important, you need to use this knowledge to create opportunities for those who have strong leadership personalities—to channel that trait into positive ways rather than negative. You'll be surprised how many discipline problems will be averted throughout the year.

20

The Multiple Intelligences Really Work

Like the last chapter, this is one on sharing some teacher methodology that I found really works.

As teachers, we use every trick in the book to reach our students. Over the years, we all learn, try, succeed, and fail with numerous innovations that we come across in our readings, observations, and in-service sessions. I believe that one of the two most useful innovations of the past thirty years is the theory of Multiple Intelligences (Cooperative Learning being the other). The Multiple Intelligences theory shows us how students think—what is it that "energizes" their brains.

Howard Gardner discovered that all of us "think" through one or more of eight different "intelligences"[1]:

- Verbal-linguistic
- Logical-mathematical
- Visual-spatial
- Bodily-kinesthetic

1 Gardner, H. (1993). *Multiple intelligences: The theory in practice.* New York: Basic Books.

- Musical
- Interpersonal
- Intrapersonal
- Naturalist

By presenting curricular material in that intelligence mode, a teacher can better "activate" the student's brain function.

I know it definitely works for me. Personally, I'm very high in the Musical Multiple Intelligence. When I'm grading the same assignments I've given for years (we haven't changed our texts in fifteen years), I like to have music on. The music "energizes" me to get through this mundane activity easier.

At the same time, this "energization" can be a distraction. I remember attending the Hollywood Bowl for a Tchaikovsky concert (my favorite classical composer), and I was having a horrible time concentrating on the music. The music was activating my brain so much that I kept getting ideas about a new book I was in the process of writing. I couldn't stop thinking about it! I finally had to start jotting down notes on my program to get the ideas out of my head so I could enjoy the music.

I won't go into a long dissertation about the Multiple Intelligences here—that could take up a book in itself, and the information is readily available.[2] Rather, I want to share a couple of non-traditional ways I've incorporated the Multiple Intelligences in the classroom.

At the beginning of the year, I give my students a simple test to determine their highest Multiple Intelligence. I mark the results in my roll book and pull out that information when

---

2 For one of the best teacher-friendly books on the Multiple Intelligences, see Armstrong, T. (2009). *Multiple intelligences in the classroom* (3rd ed.). Alexandria, VA: Association for Supervision and Curriculum Development.

needed (usually when the student is having some difficulty on some curricular concepts).

For example, let's say a student was having difficulty understanding the theme of a particular story. I'd look in my roll book to see the student's high Multiple Intelligences, and then I would do the following:

- If the student is high in Linguistic Intelligence, I would sit with the book and discuss sections of the story that directly affected or were evidence of the theme.
- If the student is high in Logical/Mathematical Intelligence, I would go to the board and make a flow chart diagraming how the various aspects of the story logically related to the theme.
- If the student is high in Spatial Intelligence, I would locate a picture or two related to the theme and describe the concepts using the picture as a guide.
- If the student is high in Bodily-Kinesthetic Intelligence, I would make up an excuse and have the student walk with me to the office while I explained the concepts, just to get the student physically moving.
- If the student is high in Musical Intelligence, I would simply play music in the background while we discussed the concepts.
- If the student is high in Intrapersonal Intelligence, I would provide the student with some questions to think about, relating to the concepts.
- If the student was high in Interpersonal Intelligence, I would assign a "buddy" to discuss the concepts with the student.

- If the student is high in Naturalistic Intelligence, I would go sit outside and discuss the concepts.

I know that this is very simplistic, and very time consuming, and I do not go through the process every time a student needs help. It's a tool I turn to when other easier and quicker methods do not seem to be effective. Most important, it's a good methodology to have at your disposal.

The other time I really incorporate the Multiple Intelligences is a bit unorthodox—but quite useful. I have used the information during our annual standardized testing.

Standardized testing has been "high stakes" for years—ever since No Child Left Behind came into existence in 2002. It's the time we really need our students to do their best, as the school and/or teachers are evaluated to some degree based on student test scores. Unfortunately, if you believe in the validity of the Multiple Intelligences, the school testing environment is essentially contrary to what energizes their thinking! Unless the student is high in Linguistic or Logical/ Mathematical Intelligences, a distinct disadvantage is present with the use of standardized testing. For those students *not* high in those two areas, this is what I do to energize their thinking for this critically important task:

- For the students who are high in Spatial Intelligence, I put up some pictures of that subject area where they can notice them, as visual representations stimulate their thought patterns. Obviously I do not post anything that would help on the test—but things in that general subject area. I also make sure that they have scratch paper to doodle on during the test (which is later collected and turned in).

- For the students who are high in Bodily-Kinesthetic Intelligence, I let them have a squeeze ball or some other manipulative device at their desk to use during the test to keep some muscles working.

- For the students who are high in Musical Intelligence, I have music playing during set-up and during breaks.

- For the students who are high in Intrapersonal Intelligence, I have them sit in the corners of the room, away from others who would distract them simply by their presence.

- For the students who are high in Interpersonal Intelligence, I have them sit next to their friends. They aren't talking or sharing answers, but the proximity of others has been shown to help them with their thinking.

- For the students who are high in Naturalist Intelligence, I have them sit facing a window, or, if that's not feasible, have them facing a plant or "classroom pet."

Some of these practices are a bit unorthodox, and it takes some explaining whenever an administrator enters the room. However, it's up to us as teachers to use whatever is at our disposal to energize our students' thinking abilities. After all, it's the teacher that too often is held accountable for the students' test scores. Why not use any advantage available to raise student scores? The Multiple Intelligences is a great tool to use in testing and other endeavors throughout the year in order to energize your students' thinking processes.

21

Make 'em Laugh

STUDENT: What time does this class end?

ME: When the bell rings.

STUDENT: When does the bell ring?

ME: At the end of the period.

STUDENT: When will that be?

ME: When I dismiss you to your next class.

This exchange can go on for another eight-to-ten questions before the student gives up. It's one of the reasons I have few classroom management problems—I can be more obnoxious than any student in my class, if need be.

My point? Sometimes you just gotta use humor to get through the "crap" a teacher needs to endure nowadays.

I use humor all of the time when I teach—both with kids and adults. Sometimes I just feel like giving out signs like Bill Engvall does in his "Here's your sign" routine (a comedy classic every teacher should listen to—but more on that later).

Humor allows you to keep your sanity in the face of an insane teaching environment. It often allows you to get your point across, or deal with an obnoxious student, without getting upset. I can't count how many times I look at my sixth-grade students and simply remark to the group, "And this is the gifted class?"

I find that bringing humor into the classroom makes the day more enjoyable—even if the work is serious. It allows you to put things into perspective and, more important, it reduces a tremendous amount of stress with your students.

From spelling tests to explanations about homework, I use humor whenever possible. Even when disciplining a student, I don't get mad. I get sarcastic. As I stated earlier, one of my students once told me, "It's not the referrals you give that upset me—it's that you're always smiling when you hand them out."

One of my favorite t-shirts to wear simply states: "DEFINE NORMAL." That's the theme of my classroom. If you're "crazy" or "weird" or "off the wall" in my room, that's considered "normal" behavior.

I regularly start off the year by informing my sixth graders that I'm from another planet. I tell them how the movie *Men in Black* was actually a documentary. (What's scary is that, if I present it well enough, some of my sixth graders actually believe me.)

April Fools' Day is a classic in my class. It's become a "rite of passage" that the kids remember from year to year. "Did Mandel get you, too?" is commonly asked in early April. This is how I set it up: On April 1, I create a reason to "get mad" at my gifted sixth graders—they haven't been putting enough effort into their work, they did lousy on a homework assignment I just graded, or something of that nature. I then give them a "surprise" test. Ten questions: I take the book and orally select very obscure items for my questions. I keep reminding them how important this test is going to be—and it will require a parent's signature if they fail. By the tenth question, they are completely panicking. The last question is always "What day is today?" I then watch the "light bulbs" start to go on in their heads as they realize that they have been had. (This past year's group then crumpled up their papers and threw them at me.)

I know what you're thinking—this is cruel. How do you think I get my reputation for being "mean and rotten"? I didn't say *they* had to feel it was funny. *I* had a good time doing it. And the seventh and eighth graders share stories with the sixth graders how I "got them" in previous years—it adds to my legacy.

As I wrote earlier, my class is always very tough academically, but I try to make it a lot of fun. You, as a teacher, need to strike that kind of balance.

The best, of course, is Halloween, which I talked about earlier, how I wore very "strange" costumes every year.

I mentioned the comic Bill Engvall earlier. My Pacoima Singers have actually adopted his "Here's Your Sign" routine. As Engvall says, it's for people when they do or say "stupid" things. Rather than getting upset with them, you give them a sign pointing it out. Here's an example of how he uses it:

> I got stuck behind a big rig that wedged his trailer underneath an overpass. And me and the trucker were standing on the side of the road talking. And a Highway Patrolman pulls up, and he looks at the guy's rig, and he looks at the trucker...and says, "You got your truck stuck?"
>
> And bless this trucker, he says, "Nope, I was delivering this overpass and I ran out of gas.
>
> "Here's your sign."

> A buddy in the Navy...he's waiting to get on his cruise ship, and he's in full Navy gear and this lady walks up to him and says, "Are you in the Navy?"
>
> And without missing a beat, he says, "No ma'am—the Village People are missing a singer and I'm just filling in for the night."
>
> "Here's your sign."[1] [Okay—you need to be over 40 to understand that one.]

When someone in my singing group says or does something really "dumb" or off the wall, the kids all shout out, "Give her a sign!" And we give the person an imaginary sign. It makes everyone laugh—including the "offender," and is really a socializing mechanism that brings the class together throughout the year. Invariably, there's one student who seems to "own" the sign throughout the year, and it makes her comments—and her—even more acceptable to the group. More important, it gives the students experience in laughing at themselves and not taking everything too seriously.

I also use humor whenever possible with adults, especially during my in-service and salary-point classes. These are generally classes or sessions where the teachers are there involuntarily, or they have to take the class in order to progress up the salary scale. As I always state at the beginning, I know that they're not there to partake of my brilliance—they're there to get salary-point credit. Humor makes it more bearable for them—and often for me.

I always start off my adult in-service sessions with this story:

---

1 Engvall, B. (2004). A decade of laughs. Audio recording. Warner Brothers.

A teacher died and went to heaven and met St. Peter, who said, "We're glad to see you here. Let me show you where you're going to live."

So he took her to the first neighborhood, and it was beautiful. The houses were gorgeous, lawns perfect, and people were everywhere having picnics and parties. The teacher was excited and asked, "Is this where I'm staying?'

St. Peter said, "No. This is for the doctors. You're a little farther."

So they walked to the next neighborhood, and like the previous one, the houses were amazing, the lawns were perfectly manicured, and people were everywhere having picnics and parties. The teacher asked, "Is this where I'm staying?"

St. Peter answered, "No—you're in the next one."

So they went to the next neighborhood, and like the previous ones, the houses were gorgeous, lawns perfect, but there was one difference—it was deserted. No one was there. The teacher was despondent, and turned to St. Peter and asked, "St. Peter, don't you get any teachers up here?"

St. Peter looked at her and answered, "Oh sure—we get a lot of them. You'll meet them tomorrow. Today, they're spending the day in hell at another in-service."

While laughing, I then start my formal presentation.

Always make 'em laugh.

22

Parents Are Your Greatest Allies

As suggested in the earlier chapters, I believe that virtually every success—or failure—you experience in education is tied to your attitude. This is especially true when dealing with relationships with parents.

Recall the story I told in my chapter on grading: I had a parent who was very upset with the grades that I was giving her elementary school child. Regardless of my "logic," regardless of the "facts" in my grade book, she was not happy and was sharing this unhappiness with my principal and myself in the principal's office. Rather than arguing, rather than getting upset, I handed her a blank report card and said, "Fill this out the way you want, and I'll sign it." The parent backed off, and I made my point.

Teachers need to remember that parents are normally very protective when their children are involved. Parents usually spend significant time and care in selecting doctors, babysitters, cribs, clothes—even who holds their child. To no one's surprise, the vast majority are naturally concerned with the care of their child when a teacher is involved. Teachers need to recognize and acknowledge that fact. We are actively dealing with the most precious commodity a parent has. It is extremely important to understand this point, especially for teachers who are not parents themselves.

At the same time, parents must remember that teachers are professionals. They have gone through years of training and usually have years of experience working in their profession. They also have a massive responsibility for the care of anywhere from 20 to 40 students in their classroom—each one deserving of their personal consideration and time. Seven hours a day, 180 days a year. A total of 1,260 hours a year. (Okay—that thought may be a bit overwhelming.)

Parents also need to recognize and acknowledge this fact.

Teachers want parents to be supportive of their educational program, and parents want teachers to care for their children's educational needs. It sounds like a perfect partnership. So why does it sometimes go wrong? Mostly because of miscommunication and mistrust. For example:

From a classroom teacher's perspective:

- A passive parent is often considered one who "doesn't care about the child's education."
- An active parent is looked upon as an "aggressive troublemaker."

From a parent's perspective:

- A teacher's "negative" actions are often looked upon as the result of "not liking my child."
- A teacher who does not excuse the student from something is giving no consideration to the child's out-of-school life.

Both perspectives are incorrect and too often stereotypical. Both sides need to work together toward a common goal: the student's increased academic achievement.[1]

I believe in a holistic approach to education. We are responsible for the overall, all-encompassing growth of the child. And by "we," I mean the teacher-parent partnership.

I personally welcome parents into my classroom and strongly encourage them to come to Back to School Night. That's when I get to sell myself and my program. It's up to you, the teacher, to educate parents on how your goal is to enrich their children, and how you're going to implement that goal. I always acknowledge their parental role and call what we have a "partnership." We are working together to reach the same goal, although we each have our own separate roles and responsibilities.

Here are a few basic concepts I incorporate into my classroom in order to make this partnership work:

Communication: I insist on two-way communication with my students' parents. As stated earlier, I provide them with my cell phone number and e-mail address. Most teachers refuse to give out their number—however, I've done it for over thirty years and it's been abused only once. As I stated earlier, I do insist on some restrictions—primarily, it is *not* to be used for homework questions. I let them know that I will, at times, inform them that this is an inappropriate use of a phone call. I also share with them that if I don't take the call, it's because I'm busy with my life. (And I tell them *never* to call during a Cleveland Browns football game.) I also let them know that e-mail is the best and preferred way to get in touch with me, and if a follow-up call is needed, I'll get right back to them.

In my thirty-plus years of utilizing this policy, I have had only *one* parent abuse it, and I had to hang up on her. Once in thirty-plus years—that's not a bad record.

1 Mandel, S. (2007). *The parent-teacher partnership: How to work together for student achievement.* Chicago: Zephyr Press.

I always make it clear to the parents that it is critical that they inform me if something traumatic occurs in the child's life. This includes deaths, divorces, and, in the case of those with behavioral difficulties, a phone call before school if their child has had a bad morning. By having this information, I can immediately prepare for potential variations in their child's normal behavior, from the time they arrive at school. It allows me to be proactive instead of reactive to problematic behaviors due to the personal trauma.

I communicate with the parent regularly throughout the year. All D's and F's on tests must be signed. Every 5-6 weeks I send home a list of work that their child is missing or has done poorly. If I do my communication job correctly, the grade on the report card is never a surprise.

I also make a deal with the parents at the beginning of the year at Back to School Night: I won't believe half of what their child says about them, if they don't believe half of what their child says about me.

Parent Conferences: I have a standard rule concerning parent conferences—the student *must* be at the conference, or I will not hold the conference (unless the child is receiving an "A"). The reason is simple—the student can't lie in front of me. When parents question my reasoning, I explain that if I give a bad report to the parent, and the parent goes home and confronts the child, is the child going to say, "Mandel's right—I did screw up on that"? No!! The child is naturally going to lie or distort the truth to get out of trouble. Especially with my gifted students—their creativity comes out quite extensively when trying to justify a negative report. However, the student can't do that when sitting in front of me at the conference.

My second rule is that if this partnership is going to work, I must make the conference accessible to the parent. Don't you hate it when the utility company says, "We'll be at your place sometime between 8 and 12 on Wednesday morning. Someone needs to be there" with no consideration of the demands on your personal time? Well, parents can't always make "assigned" conference times—especially those who work in lower socio-economic jobs that pay hourly. I've held conferences as early as 6 A.M. and as late as 6 P.M. If the conference is that important (and not all are—some can be handled in a short phone call), I'm going to make sure that it happens at a time when the parent can attend. This is a major aspect of the teacher-parent partnership.

Problem Parents: Unfortunately, not all parents are cooperative or willing to engage in a real partnership with you. Those who aren't have to be dealt with individually, usually with the advice and assistance of the administrator. Keep your professionalism high. It's critical that you know when to give in, when to compromise, and when it really isn't that important in the grand scheme of things. (How many of you are now humming the words to Kenny Rogers's "The Gambler"—"You've got to know when to hold 'em/ Know when to fold 'em/ Know when to walk away?" Okay, that song may be before your time.)

Even those of us with decades of experience sometimes deal with parents who are exasperating (for lack of a better word). Remember my opening anecdote about the parent to whom I handed a blank report card and said, "Fill it out like you want, I'll sign it." Sometimes it's just not worth the fight. This is one of the hardest decisions that a teacher has to make—when to balance one's professionalism with one's sanity.

However, with all parental interactions, I always incorporate one unbendable tenet—I do not tolerate any verbal abuse. This is an important rule for you to follow as a professional: If a parent becomes abusive, walk away; end the conference. Inform your administrator immediately, providing a *written* account of the *exact* language and incident, and the actions that the parent took. In subsequent interactions with this abusive parent, be they formal or informal conferences, it's perfectly acceptable to insist on an administrator being present in the room.

Fortunately, problem parents are a distinct minority. Unfortunately, every teacher gets at least one or two every year. It goes with the territory. However, if you treat your parents as partners in their child's educational process, they will prove to be your greatest allies, and you will reduce incidents of problem parent behavior.

Ultimately, the most important component of a successful partnership with parents is the mutual respect you demonstrate through communication, conferences, and dealing with problems. And once you've established this successful partnership, you will get the ultimate compliment from parents—not a nice gift at the end of the year (although that's always welcome), but when the parent demands that younger siblings be placed in your classroom.

23

Keeping My Sanity All These Years

People often ask me how I've kept my sanity teaching in my district for over thirty-five years. I tell them I belong to ten California wine clubs. Now, I don't recommend drinking wine as a method for teachers to keep their sanity, though it does help. Rather, there are a number of things I actually do to keep my sanity that I'm going to share here. Whereas each individual's personality is different, many of these ideas are applicable to all. Use them for what it's worth, while you develop your own methods for keeping sane while being a classroom teacher.

The most important way of keeping my sanity is talking to someone regularly. I have friends on staff that I talk to almost every day about things both at school and outside of school. For a new teacher, this is critical. When I mentor new teachers, I often pull them out of their classrooms at nutrition/recess and lunch to have them participate in the real world. Too often they are so stressed with time management and planning that they stay in their rooms during their breaks to work, thinking that it will be more stressful if they don't work every minute at their craft. Sealing yourself in the classroom with limited or no contact with your peers is probably the number-one way to produce teacher stress in the long term.

Talking to others helps in a number of ways. First, you often find that problems you're facing are universal, and not just your problems. Be they individual students or administrative mandates, when you know others are experiencing the same feelings as you are, it helps. Second, it keeps you "human"—reminding you that there is life outside of the classroom for other staff members as well.

That leads to my next recommendation—socialize with your peers at faculty-organized activities such as special lunches, parties, or a staff Happy Hour. A Friday Happy Hour is an instant stress reducer for the week. It also helps develop connections and networks among your colleagues. Even if you don't drink alcohol, you can order a soft drink or water and join in on the social engagement. That's what's important. In fact, if you ever walk into a restaurant bar on Friday afternoon and see a group of people laughing and having a great time, ask them where they teach. (I maintain that over 90% of the time they are teachers. They're enjoying each other's company and putting their stressful week into its proper perspective.)

Don't completely compartmentalize your school and private life. Be sure to talk to your significant other or outside friends about your work. To completely "wall off" your school day as your "work life" turns it into exactly that—a work environment that becomes less pleasurable as your mind classifies it as "work," and therefore more stressful and less fun.

Another way you, as a teacher, can keep your sanity is to make sure that you do things you like on a regular basis, and even integrate them into the school day when appropriate. Many of my friends on staff go to the gym every day, take yoga, or ride horses. A group of teachers at my school enjoy jogging so much that they formed an SRLA (Student Run Los Angeles) chapter for the students at our school. Every day after school, they prepare themselves and students to run in the annual Los Angeles Marathon. Many teachers have a set movie night or date night with their significant other. And I know when my principal has gone golfing on a weekend, because she's in a great mood that Monday morning. Your teaching work cannot control your life—you cannot spend ten-to-twelve-hour days and weekends grading papers and/or planning. Doing so will ensure that you burn out. Your attempt to be a "Super Hero" will actually make you less effective and/or shorten your career in the long run. Teaching is a marathon, not a sprint. Do the work you have to do, and play during the time you have to play. Oh—and as of this writing, I'm well past level 5000 on Candy Crush®. That's one of my little sanity breaks during the day.

There are a number of other things I do that help me to keep my personal sanity. For starters, I have a "personal" wall by my desk. On that wall I post things that pertain just to me. These include certificates and plaques I've been awarded over the years, pictures that have a personal special meaning, and just fun stuff I've accumulated. (For example, I have a posted sign that says, "I always wanted to be somebody, but now I realize that I should have been more specific."—Lily Tomlin.) During the week, I spend more waking hours in my "work home" than I do at my regular home! I need it to be comfortable and ... well ... "me." By making one small part "personal," I accomplish that goal.

I also have a number of personal touches around my room. I have a Cleveland Browns flag on the wall, visible when you walk in. (See Chapter 10, "Support Your Home Team," for explanation.) I have other Cleveland sports team paraphernalia around the room. These include a stool that has a Browns jersey where you sit, and two "human legs" in Browns cleats and socks as its base. (My wife won't allow it in the house, so it's here at school.)

Of course, I have all of the regular stuff posted that a good teacher has—student work, encouragement posters, and the like. But also around the room are a number of props that I've accumulated as mementos from my Singers shows over the past twenty-seven years: a mannequin wearing a Singers shirt, a large turkey leg, King Arthur's Holy Grail, a personalized Wall Drug sign, a six-foot banana, and more. This classroom is my "home away from home" for 180 days a year. It's comfortable and welcoming, and I've made it mine. You should do so with your own classroom—you'd be surprised how it helps to relax your mood and disposition.

Another thing that preserves my sanity is education jokes. I love reading them and sharing them with teachers. A number of teachers follow me on Facebook just for the jokes I post. I also love to watch humorous teacher videos on YouTube. Some of my favorites are those created by Gerry Brooks. He's a former principal who makes these hysterical "educational" videos for teachers. Google his name and enjoy some of them.

Finally, the number-one trick I've learned for keeping my sanity is the need to put things into their proper perspective. I no longer worry about things I can't change, nor do I get upset about them, either. There are a number of "pain in the neck" types of things we all have to do as teachers—paperwork, administrative directives, and repetitive meetings, just to name a few. I simply deal with them without complaining, because complaining is only going to stress me out and not change a thing. The things I *can* change, I absolutely will act on, but a lot of teacher stress comes from things that can't be changed. Don't let those things bother you. It's not worth it. Keep your focus on your students, in particular on areas where you can effect change and make a difference. You should continually ask yourself: "Will such-and-such make a difference to the success of my students?" If the answer is "No," then why stress over it?

The same rule is applicable in situations and interactions with problematic parents or students that I really can't change. I once questioned one of my principals as to why she always gave in to parental requests. Her answer was quite practical. She explained that in that area, if she didn't do what the parent wanted, the parent would go over her head to the local district. The local district would subsequently call her and order her to do what the parent originally wanted. So why fight it? I couldn't argue with that logic. Sometimes the fight isn't worth it, especially when you know it's a losing battle. Concentrate on those you can win, and limit the energy you expend on those you know you will eventually lose.

Remember the example I mentioned about giving a complaining parent a blank report card and saying, "Fill this out the way you want, and I'll sign it." It wasn't worth the fight, nor was it worth getting annoyed over.

These are a number of tactics I've used to keep my sanity over the years. Every experienced teacher has his or her individual ways of achieving the same goal. I asked a number of my teacher friends, "How do you keep your sanity while being a classroom teacher all these years?" Here are some of their responses:

LALO: I focus on those kids who really want to learn. They give me energy to be patient with others who are a little lost.

MEL: Find balance. Unplug. Make sure you have a circle of friends outside of teaching.

STEPHANIE: I volunteer on weekends with pet rescues, and playing with dogs and cats is therapeutic. And Starbucks.

KRISTIN: I exercise a lot.

JENI: Naps are good.

CHERYL: It really helps if some of your co-workers are personal friends.

KATIE: As an introvert, I read at my desk during nutrition, lunch, and sometimes before or after school. It helps me to re-center myself and get some much-needed quiet time.

KELLY: Hang out with friends who can relate and laugh it out. Actually, that's the best way to get ideas, too, for solutions to those systemic stressors.

DAN: Movies, theater, concerts, books, museums—all of the time. They make me a little stronger and I almost always come away with something to share with my students.

SEVAN: Breathing. Close your door, turn off the lights, and breathe for about 5–10 minutes.

EDDIE: Seeking out friends in the profession and forming a support system of colleagues.

ROB: Every year, I teach most topics differently or with a new approach so as to not become bored.

SHAYLEEN: I laugh with the kids every day. There are constantly funny moments, and we find humor in it all and laugh together.

All of these suggestions are helpful in that they work for that particular teacher. Ultimately, it's every teacher's responsibility to determine what to do to keep one's own sanity. I've shared just a few of the tricks I've learned over the years. They must work, since I'm still sane after all these years. Sort of.... You'll eventually discover yours, too.

24

My Retirement Plan

I sat down with a retirement specialist a couple of years ago (wanting to look into 401[k]s), and he asked me when I wanted to retire. I answered, "Never." In response to his dumbfounded look, I explained:

- I teach my hobby, Musical Theater, all day. I also teach gifted English and history. I love what I do.
- My wife and I vacation over 40 days a year; children are grown and actually financially independent (finally).
- I don't play golf.

My question to him was, "What am I going to do in retirement?"

Over spring break last year I actually spent two days doing nothing but watching TV and playing video games. I thought I was going to go out of my mind.

So, when people ask me what my retirement plan is, I refer to an object I have in the corner of my classroom.

A real coffin.

Many years ago, we were performing the "funeral song" from the show *Ragtime*. The father of one of my students was a mortician, and he donated a simple coffin for us to use in the song. I've kept it as part of my classroom décor for over twenty-five years now. (I tell the students it's part of my "discipline policy.") We've occasionally used it for haunted houses, but mostly it's a conversation piece.

I've maintained that when I finally go, I want stage crew to reinforce it and I want it used for my funeral.

Those who know me will get the joke.

25

What Have I Learned?

During one of my recent in-service classes, one of the teachers asked me, "What have you learned over the years?" I paused momentarily, as I've never been asked that question. I'd like to think that I've learned one or two things in my forty-plus years of working with kids. Most of these ideas I've already discussed in earlier chapters, but some key, special ideas bear repeating. So, in no particular order, here are ten of the most important things I've learned so far in my teaching career.

#1—Nothing is more important than knowing you've affected a child's life.

Throughout the years, I've been the only one among my friends who has always been able to say that I love my job. Most days, I can't wait to get to work. I cannot comprehend how some people can go to a 9-to-5 job they dislike every day. It would be mental torture for me.

I get a special long-term pleasure from many of my former students with whom I've stayed in contact. There was a family of three girls whom I taught in elementary school thirty-some years ago. I've gone to all three of their weddings and have been in touch with them while they've all had their own kids. There are dozens of former students I keep in touch with—ten, twenty, thirty years later. In fact, at my wedding, my wife and I had a full table of former students.

But nothing is more satisfying—and more humbling—than having a former student write a message on Facebook saying something to the order of, "I am who I am because of you." That moment makes it all worthwhile.

#2—This isn't a 9-to-5 job.

We're teachers. But we're 21st-century teachers. The job has changed dramatically in the past thirty to forty years. No longer are we just purveyors of knowledge. Now we're also pseudo parents, social workers, psychologists, and counselors. Unfortunately, in today's society, that's what the job has become.

Just this past year, I had a number of my graduating Singers thank me for being their "School Dad." We are whatever our students need us to be. And good teachers can't just turn it off when the bell rings. That's one reason I give my phone number and e-mail address to parents, and they know that their child can contact me if it's really important. (And, to repeat, I do not take homework questions.) I also let the students know they can contact me at any time if they need a "safe adult" to talk to, or if they're in trouble. About twenty years ago I had a student run away from home and call me from a rather bad neighborhood. My wife and I went out to get her. We sat with her and talked, and ultimately she let us call her parents to let them know she was safe, and then we drove her home. Now, I know that this borders on the extreme, and I'm not sure I'd do it again in today's climate. But the point is, we're here for our students, and often we have to fulfill necessary roles that go beyond the 8-to-4 time frame, and that go beyond the traditional teacher roles that we experienced when we were our students' age.

#3—It takes a special set of skills to be a middle school teacher.

I love middle school. Okay—many of you think I'm crazy to say that. The majority of teachers like the little ones, so they become elementary teachers. Or they like the older ones, and they go on to teach in high school. Few teachers voluntarily choose to go to middle school. Even among my staff—which is a very good staff—many of them would immediately grab an elementary or high school position if it were offered.

I love middle school because I see more personal development in the kids than at any other level. They come in as babies in sixth grade and leave as young adults after eighth. It's here in middle school that they develop their social skills and their personalities. In high school, they're already set in their ways—they've already developed their niches. Here, in middle school, they're still exploring.

Now, granted, this age often can put them in moods and behaviors that can drive you crazy. For example, in sixth grade, spring semester, when a social problem develops between a couple of kids, the first thing I usually ask is, "Who broke up with whom?" And often the middle school girls act as if they're auditioning for a sequel to "Mean Girls." Usually, though, the students are absolutely enjoyable as you watch them grow.

As a performing arts teacher, I've actually turned down a prestigious high school magnet arts job for one simple reason: in high school, the director works for the kids. In middle school, the kids work for the director. It's more fun that way, and I can help them grow holistically.

#4—Kids don't care how much you know, as long as they know you care.

I talked about this at length in an earlier chapter, but it bears repeating here, as it's one of the most important things I've learned over the years. This is not my quote, as you know;

rather, it comes from the former president of the National Education Association. Kids today no longer fear adults—any adults. What drives them is respect. They respect those who respect them. And nothing shows them that you respect them more than when you demonstrate that you care about them. You care about their feelings, their achievements, their personalities, their lives in and outside of school. You care about them as human beings. Nothing is more important in their minds.

#5—Be yourself & be honest.

Get to know your kids—and let them get to know you. Let them know you're human—share with them ups and downs (to a reasonable extent, obviously). If you're having a bad day, or don't feel well, tell them. That way they know if you snap at them or are not your normal jolly self, it's not their fault. If you make a mistake, say so. Show them you're human. I've bought many a class donuts the day after I unfairly got on their cases because I was not in the best place the previous day.

#6—There are no rules set in stone.

This is especially true where discipline is concerned. And cooperative groups. What works at 8 A.M. may not work at 2 P.M. What works for one class may not work for another. The kids are different, the mix different. *You're* different at various hours of the day. Rainy or windy days affect the kids. And as I related earlier, any good elementary teacher will swear to you that they can tell when it's a full moon without looking outside.

Roll with it. Have basic principles and guidelines that you follow. Always have contingencies. And sometimes, just enjoy the madness.

#7—Have fun—enjoy the kids!

This goes along with enjoying the madness. Enjoy the kids. They're unique, and usually fun. Enjoy Fridays. My students know I'm in a great mood on Friday, that nothing bothers me that day. And unless they have a test, it's usually a light day. It's my way of getting them ready for the adult work world and appreciating Fridays. I always say, "I'm a teacher; I love Fridays."

#8—Administrators want you to succeed.

I love when administrators come into my room for a visit. It gives me a chance to show off what we're doing. I don't know why so many teachers are afraid of their administrators and panic when they enter the room or sit in for an observation.

It makes no sense for administrators not to want you to succeed. They *do* want you to succeed! Having successful teachers makes them look good, and when you succeed, you're one less problem for them. If you're doing a special lesson, invite them in. Ask them for advice. Even if you don't use it, you'll sometimes get some good tips and they'll feel appreciated.

At every interview I've told my prospective principal something my father once taught me: My job is to make the principal look good. The more I make the principal look good, the more freedom and support I get to do it.

#9—Always put things in perspective.

With the craziness that's going on in public education, with the regulations, the rules, the paperwork, the obsession with and pressure of testing, there's one thing I've learned that has kept my sanity more than anything else: Keep everything in perspective. In other words:

> Blow off what needs to be blown off.
> Do what needs to be done.
> Enjoy the rest.

Some things just aren't important enough to fret over, and you need to recognize what they are. Sometimes you just have to do "teacher work" whether you like it or not, since it's part of the job. Just like any job. Do it and don't stress over it. Once you get those negative things out of your mind, you're left with the positives and fun. Concentrate on those. 'Cause I guarantee—you ain't doing this job for the money!

#10—"Love is good, hate is bad, see you tomorrow."

As I wrote in the beginning of this book, John Jacobson shared this quote from his father, and it's become my personal motto. Even more so now.

Three summers ago I had a massive heart attack while on vacation (this after almost dying from cancer six years before). The only reason I'm alive, I've been told, is because there was an off-duty EMT standing next to me who called his buddies, and they immediately got me to a hospital. Prior to this, I was at no risk of a heart attack. If I had been home, I would have lain down and never woken up. I would have been one of those stories about a guy in great health dropping dead. It very much put things into perspective for me. And that especially includes my job.

I have no time for negative energy. Since my heart attack, I enjoy my students more than I have for years. My classes are more fun. My school is more enjoyable. To this day, after over forty years in the classroom, I can honestly say that I still love my job.

Love is good. Hate is bad.

And I know we teachers will continue educating children. I know we'll continue being important in shaping kids' lives. That's what we do.

See you tomorrow.

References

Armstrong, T. (2009). *Multiple intelligences in the classroom* (3rd ed.). Alexandria, VA: Association for Supervision and Curriculum Development.

Engvall, B. (2004). *A decade of laughs.* Audio recording. Warner Brothers.

Gardner, H. (1993). *Multiple intelligences: The theory in practice.* New York: Basic Books.

Josephson, M. (2002). *Making ethical decisions.* Los Angeles: Josephson Institute of Ethics.

Lee, S. (1962). *Amazing Fantasy #15.* New York: Marvel Comics.

Mandel, S. (2003). *Cooperative work groups: Preparing students for the real world.* Thousand Oaks, CA: Corwin Press.

Mandel, S. (2007). *The parent-teacher partnership: How to work together for student achievement.* Chicago: Zephyr Press.

Mandel, S. (2009). *The new teacher toolbox: Proven tips and strategies for a great first year* (2nd ed.). Thousand Oaks, CA: Corwin Press.